ELEMENTS OF THE HELPING PROCESS: A GUIDE FOR CLINICIANS
Raymond Fox, PhD

SOME ADVANCE REVIEWS

"A theoretically integrative, people-oriented, and jargon-free guide for the therapeutic helper. Whether psychotherapist, counselor, or social worker, the reader can benefit from the concrete, creative methods which Dr. Fox describes. I would unhesitatingly recommend this for beginning clinicians."

Phyllis Rosen, PhD
Certified Psychologist, Private Practice
New York City

"At last — a how-to manual that includes why, who, and when. . . . One of the most comprehensive books written for the clinician. . . . This book should be mandatory reading for anyone interested in doing this work, or who is already in it. Its refreshing outlook and clarity deserve its constant use both as a text and source of inspiration. . . . It will guarantee that all clinicians will be able to function to their highest potential. And what more could our clients ask of us?"

Lucille Rosen, CSW, CAC, NCAII
Director, Healing Process Workshops
Hicksville, New York

Elements
of the Helping Process
A Guide for Clinicians

HAWORTH Social Work Practice
Carlton Munson, DSW, Senior Editor

Elements
of the Helping Process
A Guide for Clinicians

Raymond Fox, PhD

The Haworth Press
New York • London • Norwood (Australia)

The Haworth Press, Inc., 10 Alice Street, Binghamton, NY 13904-1580

Library of Congress Cataloging-in-Publication Data

Fox, Raymond.
    Elements of the helping process : a guide for clinicians / Raymond Fox.
        p.   cm.
    Includes bibliographical references and index.
    ISBN 1-56024-156-X (alk paper)–156024-157-8 (pbk : alk paper).
    1. Psychotherapy. 2. Counseling. 3. Helping behavior. I Title.
    [DNLM: 1. Counseling–methods. 2. Physician-Patient Relations. W 62 F793c]
RC480.F654   1992
158'.3–dc20
DNLM/DLC
for Library of Congress   92-1457
                                                                              CIP

To Jeri, my wife, with love and gratitude
for her wisdom, strength, help, and friendship.

With special thanks to:

my super children, Tracy and Tom, who tolerated my insanity
and helped restore my sanity;

MaryAnn Quaranta, Dean, Fordham University Graduate
School of Social Service, who provided both opportunity and
encouragement;

Roberta Sauerman, who supplied her creative ideas and
graphic designs; and

my students for their continual inspiration and support.

ABOUT THE AUTHOR

Raymond Fox, PhD, is Professor at Fordham University School of Social Service. A certified individual, family, group, and sex therapist maintaining a private practice, he has published extensively in the professional literature. Dr. Fox conducts workshops nationally and internationally, and is a consultant to a number of public and private agencies. He is a member of the National Association of Social Workers, the American Association of Marriage and Family Therapy, the Society of Clinical Social Work Psychotherapists, and the American Orthopsychiatric Association.

CONTENTS

9/10

Chapter I

To Do Our Work

Experience is the child of thought and thought is the child of action. We cannot learn men from books.

— Disraeli

Any beginning, any new understanding in life causes simultaneous feelings of hope and fear.

— Ruth Smalley

WHY THIS BOOK?

A clinician for the past twenty-five years and a teacher, consultant and trainer for the past fifteen years, I have come to appreciate the need for a common-sense and down-to-earth approach to the helping process. Students and colleagues who are learning ask often for direction in finding a practical guide; but what they find — and find wanting — is a literature of long scholarly treatises on theory, extended descriptions of therapeutic technique, and overblown reports on clinical research about effective intervention. Complaining that none of these offers very much usable information about how to work with people on a day-to-day basis, they go on looking for a book to fill the gaps. Theoretical frameworks and findings from research studies provide only limited help in learning the art and craft of helping. Between the ideas that science provides and the kinds of decisions the clinician must make there is a gulf that we must bridge before action can be taken.

Clients are particular and unique in nature and character. Theory is general. The fit between the two is never perfect; nor is a strong skill base enough, for a creative leap must be made if we are to

1

cross the space between often inapplicable theory and the concrete reality we face every day.

Clinicians, both new and experienced, seek practical guidelines, systematic direction and suggestions for creatively working with their clients. They need help in answering difficult questions, which include: What do I tell clients about myself? How do I divide my focus in the beginning between establishing a relationship, developing a contract, and giving the client something concrete on which to establish a basis of hope? Just how is hope instilled? How can I enhance the process and avoid getting in the way? How do I connect with clients? How do I utilize non-verbal interactions?

This book will help us confront these questions and fill the gap in the literature. It is a practical guide to working clinically with people through the various phases of the helping process. "User-friendly," it describes some familiar tried-and-true techniques but also concentrates on innovative methods of help-giving. Even though there are computer programs for learning these skills, it seems to me that computers — as valuable as they are — fall short, for they cannot provide human connection, the most essential dimension in the helping process. Even though you "cannot learn men from books," books do serve, next to person-to-person contact, as handy and discriminating means to reflection and introspection. Although there is a tendency to disparage pragmatic tools for clinical practice, what we value most in our work is the *application* of sound principles. The ultimate test of theory is its usability in actual, direct, face-to-face transactions with clients.

This book, then, differs from other textbooks in several respects. Even though it endeavors to blend theory and practice, it is not typically scholarly and does not emphasize the "science" of our work. Nor is it restricted to "left brain" conceptual and statistical elements of the work, even though theory, analysis and logic are essential ingredients of the mix. The "art" of the work is stressed instead, with "right brain" attributes of synthesis, intuition and wholeness. No reductionistic formulas or mechanical strategies are offered; but sensible tips, guidelines, "rules of thumb" and new ideas for proceeding are given.

Different from other textbooks because it does not elaborate extensively on any one school of clinical practice, *Elements of the*

Helping Process: A Guide for Clinicians is integrative in the kindest sense of the word, describing sundry theories only as they pertain to, illuminate, or explain the more immediate clinical interaction. It seeks to identify theory that fits clients at different points — and under different circumstances — during the work, and focuses especially on finding the most instrumental and relevant interventions. As we encourage a less rigid and more fluid and personal approach to clinical practice, an approach which, informed by theory and practice, opens the way for us, we respond appropriately, differentially and effectively to a wide range of clients with a broad array of problems. We have to walk the tightrope between overidentification and excessive detachment, while tailoring our work to our clients rather than expecting them to fit our approach.

Using an informal tone, I try to speak directly to "you" rather than addressing myself to some anonymous clinician. This personal style reflects directly my bias about what I believe the work can be.

This book resembles others in the field in drawing from examples from actual practice for clinical illustrations. These are selected to be instructive about intervention and to illuminate the application of theory. I have concentrated on an array of theoretical and practical approaches that characterize each stage of the helping process. A repertoire of varied suggestions and techniques are offered, encouraging you to discover your own style. We move from the engagement stage to termination, while including special chapters devoted to creative practice methods. Interventive procedures adapted to clients' discrete needs are identified, discussed and illustrated. Ways to individualize clinical practice are suggested.

GENERAL OUTLINE OF THE BOOK

The book's focus and intent are discussed in this chapter, which also takes up some of my assumptions about the helping process, along with some basic propositions about the people we call clients. I argue for an integrated approach to clinical practice and conclude with a discussion of the need for you to be an active participant rather than a passive observer in the helping process. The second chapter presents some fundamental principles and novel ideas about beginning the helping process and educating clients about the nature of helping, while making possible the deeper purpose of their reviewing their life stories. Phases of preparation for the initial contact are addressed. The chapter underscores the importance of responding to clients' valid need for structure and devotes considerable attention to what you can expect from clients and what clients expect from you. I conclude with a checklist for guiding your reflections on your work.

Creating a "Safehouse" for clients is the theme of the third chapter. The "Safehouse" is a powerful metaphor for the helping process that clarifies and unifies such diverse clinician characteristics as empathy, good rapport, neutrality and anonymity and the real and transferred relationship. Clients' growth and the ability to master internal conflict and external frustration require that you establish a setting which meets their basic needs for security and affirmation. Guidelines are laid out for building such a "Safehouse" for clients. We draw upon attachment/separation theory and elaborate upon the concept of the "holding environment."

In the fourth chapter I discuss basic philosophy, premises and principles of goal-setting and contracting. An outline for developing a sound contract is followed by an illustration from actual practice. The chapter reviews the benefits of contracting from the perspective of assessment and evaluation.

The fifth chapter focuses attention on the dynamics of the helping relationship, while stressing the centrality of "relationship" and your own awareness of self. Seven levels of relationship, the seven "I's" — as I call them — are discussed: Individualization, Intellectual learning, Imitation, Internalization, Identification, Idealization, and Individuation. The final message of the chapter is that the essence of the helping process may not be the truth arrived at as much as it is the manner of arriving at the truth.

"Learning from a Jig-saw Puzzle" is the metaphor that rules Chapter VI, where we examine the assessment process. I review what assessment is and is not, while offering guidelines for feedback, and discuss the types and general process of assessment. A section on "labeling" concludes this chapter.

Chapters VII and VIII interface with each other, for each uses the same case study to illustrate the benefit of integrating individual and family approaches. Chapter VII concentrates on individual diagnosis, examining the place of *The Diagnostic and Statistical Manual of The American Psychiatric Association III-R.* We review the theoretical underpinnings and various dimensions of individual assessment. Chapter VIII presents various facets of family assessment and proposes the Genogram as a useful tool for either individual or family assessment.

In Chapter IX, "Creative Ways of Capturing the Life Story," I explain the importance of and guidelines for discovering the client's life story. Two particular methods that I utilize in my own practice are amplified upon: the family tree and the inventory. Both are illustrated with specific examples.

Chapter X stresses the written word in the helping process, a seldom discussed, but valuable, adjunct. The usefulness of several forms of writing is detailed, showing how they crystallize a helping relationship, uncover sources of behavior and facilitate deepened understanding between you and your clients. The advantages of clients' and your own independent writing are demonstrated, even as the utility of writing as a form of interchange is shown.

The final chapter is devoted to the termination process, explaining how termination can be viewed as crisis intervention and suggesting checkpoints for clients' readiness for ending. It elaborates upon the "separation paradox" and upon three distinct, but overlapping, phases of termination.

A PARADIGM EMPHASIZING CLIENT HEALTH AND STRENGTHS

This book moves away from the typically orthodox methods of help-giving with which you may be familiar. A simplified comparison illuminates the differences between the traditional view and my more integrative one:

Traditional Emphasis	Integrative Emphasis
Theory centered	Client centered
One specialized set of orthodox techniques	Combination of approaches and techniques
External direction and rules	Inner listening and attentiveness

Emphasis on intellect and analysis	Fresh appreciation of intuition and imagination
Focus on symptoms or problems	Focus on the whole person
Fixed and rigid	Flexible and adaptable
Clinician neutral and essentially passive	Clinician active, caring and supportive
Primary intervention is interpretation	Interpretation is combined with a full armamentarium of active techniques
Client is dependent	Client is autonomous
Clinician is authority	Clinician is partner
Change in thinking, feeling or behavior is the goal	Transformation and an experience of deep healing is the goal
Primary reliance on left brain functioning of both client and clinician	Special reliance on right brain functioning of both client and clinician
Fit the client to the approach	Customize the approach to the client

BASIC BELIEFS ABOUT PEOPLE

A humanistic view, coupled with a strong dose of empathy plays the most significant role in our work. An encounter where the client is seen as a whole person through the lens of a person-to-person professional relationship underpins the success of the entire helping process.

A dozen beliefs guiding my own practice are:

1. People exist in a continually changing and sometimes incomprehensible world of experience. They struggle constantly to make sense of it and seldom give in or give up.
2. People respond to this world as they perceive it; thus their "reality" is meaningful and purposeful for them. It is neither

totally random nor absurdly ridiculous. They endeavor to find consistency in their thinking, feeling and behaving.

3. As a result of interaction with the world, and particularly with significant others, people's "self" is formed. They endeavor to be authentic and self-determining.

4. People want to be active participants in designing their lives and are dissatisfied with settling passively for their "lot in life." They recognize, to a large extent, that self-respect and self-esteem come from accepting responsibility for their lives and earning their way in the world.

5. People strive to create meaningful relationships with respectful and reliable others, whom they try not to deceive, harm or suck dry.

6. Peoples' selves are distinct and unique and cannot be pigeonholed.

7. Our strengths and capacities to regenerate our minds, bodies and emotions prevent us from being just a bundle of defects, deficits and arrests.

8. People aspire to independence and freshness while welcoming challenge. They do not ruminate repeatedly on "unfinished business" but can search out and achieve difficult objectives.

9. Progress is made in inexplicable circular spirals, for people are not simply the products of static, clear-cut, linear development.

10. People are prospective, not merely retrospective, and can influence the future and redesign their worlds, edit their scripts and exercise new options, without simply being victims of past history.

11. People are actors on the stage of life, not merely an audience. Seeking mastery and self-respect, they face unpleasant and inevitable difficulties.

12. Multi-motivational rather than uni-motivational, people make what seem to them to be the best choices at any given moment in time and are willing to exert great effort and endure considerable hardship to attain happiness.

THE PURPOSE OF CLINICAL PRACTICE

Our goal, then, is to offer people release from their suffering, encouragement for their striving, and support for their strengths. In the end, such a positive perspective promotes change. Figure 1 illustrates the purpose of clinical practice.

Promoting client autonomy and fulfillment is the overarching purpose of clinical practice. Through the integrative power of the helping relationship you communicate to clients your willingness to understand their unique qualities and you convey the expectation that their troubles can be explored and contained. As the meaning of clients' unique stories and dynamic patterns is grasped, creative interventions lead not only to resolution of problems, but to their continued growth and independence.

THE INTEGRATED APPROACH

Human experience is so rich, complex, and multi-faceted that no single theory can explain it. When drawing on many theories and methodologies, we have a greater chance to respond more fully to the range of client behavior. Breadth in viewpoint, greater flexibility in response and efficacy in intervention are increased.

The helping process includes three dimensions:

1. The helping context.
2. The client.
3. You, the helper.

This book will make it possible for you to address each dimension with increasing confidence, drawing from a broad array of theories, strategies and techniques to make you better able to create a climate of trust and to match your intervention to your clients' special needs. It offers you ways to keep clients working at tolerable levels of frustration by responding to their desire to be accepted and understood on their own terms. You are encouraged to display maximum empathy and minimum confrontation, while sustaining sufficient anxiety in the client to get to most of the core issues that are raised. You are the significant variable in influencing each of these components: the context, the client and yourself. You have your

FIGURE 1. The Purpose of Clinical Practice

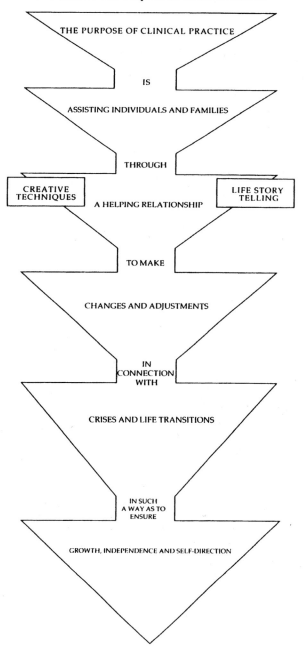

THE PURPOSE OF CLINICAL PRACTICE

IS

ASSISTING INDIVIDUALS AND FAMILIES

THROUGH

CREATIVE TECHNIQUES   A HELPING RELATIONSHIP   LIFE STORY TELLING

TO MAKE

CHANGES AND ADJUSTMENTS

IN CONNECTION WITH

CRISES AND LIFE TRANSITIONS

IN SUCH A WAY AS TO ENSURE

GROWTH, INDEPENDENCE AND SELF-DIRECTION

own personal style of helping, based on life history and personality. As you absorb new knowledge and experiment with new techniques, you will assimilate them into your own developing style. When we take an active role in genuinely collaborating with clients, we effectively interrupt dysfunctional processes that perpetuate their troublesome behavior, feeling or thinking. This book examines in detail the aspects of the work, here divided into separate spheres that, in reality, overlap and spiral.

Clinician tasks in the beginning phase are:

1. Conveying a caring attitude and an understanding of clients' pain and distress.
2. Establishing and maintaining rapport by understanding the dynamics of the helping relationship and the initial phase of clinical work, adjusting yourself to the style, language, tone and tempo of your clients.
3. Gathering information and making accurate individual and family assessments by using verbal, written, nonverbal and other data sources to identify issues, strengths and direction.
4. Educating clients about the helping process itself and providing practical information appropriate to their specific needs so as to relieve them of some of the burden they are carrying alone.
5. Contracting to prioritize targets of attention, agreeing on mutual goals, roles, tasks and timetable to work toward solutions; setting the structure for the working alliance and continually evaluating progress.
6. Motivating clients to be committed to their transformation.

Clinician tasks in the middle phase are:

7. Working "with" rather than "on" clients.
8. Clarifying misconceptions and creating an ongoing internal and external safehouse.
9. Convincing clients that you understand their suffering and are capable of helping them.
10. Recognizing clients as their own best key resource.
11. Creating resources by flexibly providing experiences for

mastery, connection with supportive others and practice in new skills.

12. Creating individualized techniques designed to match the clients' style and their situation.

13. Reinforcing clients' own competence, strengthening their coping patterns and increasing their ability to solve problems without assistance in the future.

Clinician tasks in the ending phase are:

14. Translating understanding into action that becomes part of ongoing and future experience; generalizing changes and new learnings so that they automatically become part of clients' repertoire of coping skills.

15. Dealing with forces that block learning and create barriers to action; anticipating and planning for both positive and negative consequences of change.

16. Preparing for ending the helping relationship and advancing through the phases of separation.

17. Adjusting to irremediable conditions.

18. Terminating the process of analyzing and resolving dependency issues and helping clients to achieve as much independence and assertiveness as possible; stabilizing gains and saying good-bye.

Chapter II

When You Begin,
Begin at the Beginning

To let a beginning be a beginning, to *further* its being a beginning in all its tentativeness and awkwardness, rather than to rush to solve all the problems in the first interview calls for knowledge and disciplined skills in a process that is truly professional.

— Ruth Smalley

He did not start forward to seize on my slightest pause, to assert an understanding of something before the thought was finished, or to argue with a swift irresistible impulse — the things which often make dialogue impossible.

—Anne Rice

Why are initial interviews so important? A simple answer is that there in no second chance to make a first impression. While a first impression may not be lasting, it certainly influences whatever follows and is critical because it prefigures the entire helping experience.

Poorly planned and hastily conducted first contacts frequently result in failure. This makes sense: when clients do not feel understood, they do not return. When they do feel attended to and accepted, they do come back, with even more motivation to be involved.

Take time. Listen actively. Observe selectively. Being present and available, you show your understanding and make possible a successful engagement.

Identify clients' strengths as well as problems. Recognize contextual factors in addition to internal dynamics. If you do, clients will likely return, having already sampled an effective model for your ongoing work together.

The initial interview lays the foundation for the total helping process. You and your client advance through a series of interactions forming a microcosmic model of what is ultimately to be built. Together you design what follows and structure the basic framework of the relationship. You participate in a time-limited, exploratory partnership that clarifies two situations: the one troubling the client, for which the client is seeking help; and the one in which you discover whether you can work as a team.

In the initial interview you offer the client a chance to present hurts, defeats, and problems. Different clients, of course, act differently: various behaviors are highlighted. Some clients minimize problems; some act helpless; some get blustery and aggressive; some present themselves as wronged. Their unique ways of behaving and reacting both to you and to the interview give you a sample of how they handle themselves, their feelings and the problems. This previews the way they will undertake the bigger job. Each feature and each reaction to you and to the interview foreshadows how they will react in the future. In other words, the first interview offers you a chance to learn firsthand about your clients' prospects for partnership. How capable are they? How do they handle themselves in this trial run? What personality characteristics, patterns of behavior, and decision-making abilities do they display as they explain themselves to you?

This initial encounter naturally offers clients an opportunity to assess you and determines whether you understand their suffering and whether *your* tools will be useful for what *they* want fixed or want to build. Do not forget that clients are measuring you as well as your work with them for this short time. They try to get a sense of how apt a partner you would be in helping them repair or reconstruct their lives. How do you react to them? How comfortable do you feel with them? Do you have the equipment it will take to assist them? Can they work with you? Can you work with them?

While initial interviews are geared to identifying clients' problems, making problems less confusing, and enabling clients to assume responsibility for resolving them, they also have a deeper purpose. This purpose is to provide clients with an emotionally corrective, non-judgmental experience of true acceptance, respect and hope; a collaborative experience of being heard and understood in a way that leads to purposeful and goal-directed activity.

This is a large order. Is it possible to accomplish this in a few contacts? It is, when time and thought and compassion are present. The poet understands this. Consider these words from Robert Frost:

A TIME TO TALK

When a friend calls to me from the road
And slows his horse to a meaning walk,
I don't stand still and look around
On all the hills I haven't hoed,
And shout from where I am, "What is it?"
No, not as there is a time to talk.
I thrust my hoe in the mellow ground,
Blade-end up and five feet tall,
And plod: I go up to the stone wall
For a friendly visit.

The remainder of this chapter proposes, in not-so-poetic ways — some tried and true, some new and creative — to make initial interviews more successful. It attempts to answer some questions you might have about initial interactions with clients. These common-sense questions are: Should I sit close or at a distance from the client? Should I touch the client? Should I sit behind a desk? Do I accept at face value what the client says or do I look for deeper meanings? To what should I direct attention — content, interaction, details of appearance? What should receive priority? How do I expand on minimal information? Should I ask questions or make comments? Should I keep quiet and wait for the client to begin, or should I make some opening remarks?

PREPARING FOR FIRST CONTACTS

Prepare for your clients. It is worth the effort. Preparation occurs in phases — tuning in, setting the stage, warming-up, and deciding to listen.

Tuning-In

Before actually meeting the client, review whatever information you have available about him or her. Read reports from phone contacts, from intake interviews with other people, or from other collateral sources. Talk to those who know your client. Reflect on all the information. Shelve it for a short while.

It has been argued that it is better to see a client without being swayed beforehand by the possibly biased opinions of others. A critical look at available information, however, provides a counterpoint for reflection. The more knowledge you have, the greater your chance of being able to address the client responsibly. The more knowledge you have, the better able you are to consult, consider and confront your own and others' impressions and interpretations. On the one hand, you can take stock of your own prejudices and preconceived ideas about the problem or the person. On the other, you have an opportunity to evaluate and contain stereotypes and to forestall premature conclusions or snap judgments.

Intelligent understanding allows you to be free beforehand to enter the rhythm of the exchange, to be more fully present to the client. Advance information also furnishes you with an opportunity for anticipatory empathy, a chance to walk a mile, as it were, in the client's shoes.

Advance information helps you to clarify the purpose of the initial interview. It also helps you to formulate a focus. Then, too, a little preliminary research helps you to get a clear sense of what you know, what you do not know, and what you should find out. It enables you to gear up to select the best approach to making a difference. It gives you an opportunity to determine what you can offer and ascertain the limits of what you can provide.

Setting the Stage

If you can do so, provide a private, quiet and comfortable place to sit alone with your client; physical space is a central component in creating a helping environment. Avoid interruptions for either the client or yourself. Abrupt breaks in the flow of serious dialogue, such as a telephone's nonstop ringing or an incessant pounding on the door, are distracting. Picking up the phone or opening the door is worse. Beyond being an annoyance, it disrupts any meaningful exchange between you and the client and short-circuits the natural flow of communication. Endeavor to minimize the intrusions. Post a "Do not disturb!" sign on your doorknob. Have your calls relayed. Turn off the bell on the phone. Intrusions steal precious time, depriving the client of your full and undivided attention.

Warming Up

The initial contact really begins well in advance of actually sitting down with the client. Preliminary arrangements such as appointment-setting or brief preinterview telephone conversations are stepping stones toward building a solid foundation. Lay the ground work for optimizing the initial face-to-face contact. When you make an appointment, do your utmost to keep it; if you cannot keep it, call the client promptly. Be punctual for the appointment. Cordial preliminary exchanges, all too often neglected, set a tone. Greet the client. Treat him or her receptively. Shake their hands and give your name. Invite them into your office. Observe the common courtesies. Do not treat the client in a stilted "hands-off" manner: this is simply callous. Show the reasonable human response which any person inevitably expects from another. The client is a *person* first. Particularly because this *person* happens to be a *client* in the context of a professional relationship, kind and civilized amenities ought to be observed. Treating the client in this way will put him or her at ease. More important, the client's sense of worth and dignity will be enhanced. This is an exceptionally productive way to begin.

Take an active role in initiating and maintaining the interaction. Seek to reduce emotional distance. Endeavor to reduce physical distance created by barriers to easy conversation; your desk and the client's chair should not be separated by more than five feet. Induct the client into the process. Reduce ambiguity. Let clients know how much time they will be spending with you and how much time remains in the interview as you proceed. Let them know how frequently you might be seeing them. Reduce embarrassment, irritation, and suspicion. Take nothing for granted. Prepare for the extent to which the client is experienced or knows what you expect of him or her and what he or she may expect of you. Acquaint the client with regular procedures and simple routines, such as being announced, confirming appointments, and filling out forms. Taking the time to explain the reasons for all these practices (second nature to you but foreign to your client) reduces unnecessary anxiety and elicits cooperation.

Deciding to Listen

Listen attentively. It is time to be, as the saying goes, "all ears." Probably the most common problem in communication is the failure to attend fully to what is being said so that you miss the core message. Every communication needs some degree of clarification because it is so complex. Recognize that what clients hear may not be what you say, and that what clients think they hear may be distorted. Remember that what they mean as they respond may be different from what they actually say, and that what you hear them say may differ from what they have actually said.

Listening is an active and selective process, the major component of your job. Listening is more than just listening. By your selection of words and actions, you inspire telling. To listen is to observe and sometimes to encourage. To listen is to highlight latent material for yourself and perhaps for your client. To listen requires coming to terms with and seeking to eliminate blocks to communication for the client, for yourself, and for your mutual transactions. Barriers to communication hurt the relationship, producing resentment and defensiveness. These barriers include ordering, threatening, criticizing, lecturing, blaming, and shaming. Briefly stated, then, to listen is to assemble and integrate a comprehensive picture of the forces at work within the client, within yourself and within the interaction. Your commitment to listen is primary.

Be flexible in your preparations. Once the session begins, the interaction and attentiveness to who the client *is*, and what he or she says takes precedence over whatever plans you made. Ironically, preparation makes such flexibility possible because structure encourages spontaneity.

WHAT YOU CAN EXPECT FROM CLIENTS IN THE FIRST CONTACT

At first clients are uncertain, ambivalent, and reluctant. Why shouldn't they be? Many people may have told the client that they "only wanted to help," but instead have ended by criticizing, teasing, deceiving, tricking, bullying, threatening, taunting, degrading, or manipulating. Parents may have humiliated, neglected or abused them, only for "their own good." Teachers shamed or flunked them, thinking they were helpful. Caseworkers abandoned them. I recently spoke to a foster child who had been in seven foster homes over the previous two years, all arranged by *eight* different caseworkers. There are countless horror stories (I fear many of them are true) of how different "therapists"—psychiatrists, psychologists, social workers—all in the name of "help," became instead "the rapists" who further devalued, and even molested their clients. Indeed, a social work student recently came to see me for a "consultation." He reported how his therapist dusted her office during the interview. In "only trying to help," she would slap his hand if he wept.

It is not so hard to comprehend, then, that even though they are hurting, even though they need help, clients alternate between seeking help and rejecting it. Their reserve is seldom revealed in a direct manner. Clients need and deserve your patience and perseverance.

Clients are initially wary, fearful, not ready to acknowledge openly their emotional unrest and turmoil. It is difficult enough for them to acknowledge the need for help to themselves, let alone to a stranger. Furthermore, there are cultural injunctions against allowing these feelings to be internally recognized or expressed to others (e.g., "Keep a stiff upper lip!"; "Pull yourself up by your bootstraps"). The common belief, still prevalent, is that people should be independent. Asking for help is equated with weakness, perhaps even with being "bad." Clients need your assurance and support.

In the beginning, clients may expect you to direct them. They want answers. They want quick results. Who does not? We live in an age of instants — coffee, soup, advice. Why not expect instant relief? They do not see the helping process as a joint exploration. Much has been imposed; they have been repeatedly told when to think, what to feel, how to behave. Clients need your partnership. Without theirs, you cannot proceed. You have to tell them that. Your office is not the traditional "fix-it" shop. They cannot leave their psyches behind and come back another day to pick them up.

Clients fear rejection; they fear loss of autonomy; they dread others knowing their disgrace. Recall a time when you yourself had to face rejection, admit failure, or hide shame. Recall a time when you could not resolve your problem alone; when you broke down and had to ask for help. What was it like to request help? Were you frightened? Humiliated? Lucid? Overwhelmed? Trusting? Did you want instant relief or introspective reflection? Could you talk easily to the other? Or did you test the other first to measure if he or she was genuinely interested and could be trusted? Did you consciously distort some of the facts? Unconsciously censor some? Looking back, did you succeed in deceiving yourself and perhaps the helper?

Clients seek help because something has gone wrong. They are frightened, and need your interest and compassion. When you show these, they more easily disclose their troubles and more willingly recount their life story.

Clients' hesitancy and wariness, often dubbed "resistance," are expectable and revealing responses that hint at their life story. Do not treat their reactions as resistance. When you do, you will usually alienate them further, and in many instances, "blame the victim."

Endeavor to get past complaints. Yes, something has gone miserably wrong. But if you get stuck in resultant conditions — symptoms, if you will — although these are relevant, little will change. Clients have a story to tell, one that is integrally connected to their problems. Encourage them to tell it.

Do not define your clients simply by the sum total of their problems, deficiencies, injuries. Your work, at its most effective, goes beyond a strict focus upon their bundle of problems. Rather, it encompasses some attempt at fathoming their life story. Clients have enormous anxiety, however, about telling it. Recognize that they want to protect themselves against even their own recognition . . . to present themselves to you in the best possible light . . . to defend against your labels and anticipated denouncement . . . to preserve some sense of integrity and dignity. Recognize all this and respect them for it.

Clients come to the initial session with a variety of attitudes and behaviors. Some clients appear too "comfortable" (e.g., clients who repeatedly return to talk to you about their problems as a substitute for self-reliant action or outside relationships). Some clients act "cool," others behave angrily. Expect diversity in the way clients respond during first interviews. Always keep in mind, however, that it is hard to ask for help — sometimes even harder to receive it.

It is hard to open up to an intimate associate — even harder to open up to a stranger.

It is hard to view yourself honestly and clearly — even harder when you are exhausted, overwhelmed, guilty, or ashamed.

It is hard to be composed when under internal stress — even harder when external pressure is relentless.

It always takes courage to confront who you are and where you came from — whether voluntarily or not.

It takes plain "guts" to review, edit and attempt to rewrite your life story.

If you respect who clients *are* and hear them thoroughly, you will achieve the goal of the first interview. They will return for the second.

WHAT CLIENTS EXPECT FROM YOU

One of the most common errors you can make is to rush the process along without giving clients ample opportunity to reveal their story and have a chance to assimilate the experience of being in a new kind of relationship. An old adage, "Fools rush in where wise men fear to tread," is apropos here. Try not to leap to conclusions without first appreciating the client's perceptions and feelings.

Clients have certain reasonable expectations for you during the first contacts. These include expectations of initiating and maintaining communication between them and yourself, of being sensitive to their tension and discomfort, and of structuring interviews.

Open the door to communication. Clients are on your "turf." They need to be invited in and given the opening for talking. Consciously decide to allow clients to express themselves by guiding conversation along paths that let them determine whether or not and to what degree they are going to be able to express troubled feelings and thoughts. You can enhance a sense of welcome by being there "for" the client in a caring but nonsentimental way. Assign importance to what they present and avoid any temptation to pressure for what they are not able or willing to say. You will not be able to convince them that you are trustworthy or expert unless you behave in a way that shows that you are. No matter how often you assure them you can be trusted, it means nothing unless your demeanor matches your words.

When clients begin to open up, be silent for a while to see where the spontaneous flow goes without letting them get lost. Provide verbal (e.g., "Please explain that last point further," "Tell me which of these issues you find to be most frustrating," "Come back to your feelings about your oldest daughter") and nonverbal (e.g., nodding your head, extending your open palm, smiling) encouragement so that they know what to focus on. To begin where *they* are is to communicate in an array of ways that you are with them — which is precisely what they should expect of you. Check and correct your perception as you move along. For example, "Is what I hear you saying . . .?"; "Am I correct in thinking that you feel confident about yourself when you are able to confront your wife?"; "At this moment, you seem sad to me; am I seeing you accurately?" In this way you develop a model of reciprocity. Convey, "I want to know who you are. I want to know as much as possible about you so that I can tailor our work to your unique situation and strengths." Customize your approach to clients' discrete and individual styles.

"Being with" clients is shown by active involvement with them in the process — setting a climate of acceptance and concern, clarifying, suggesting new perspectives, and being sensitive to boundaries and limitations. It involves encouraging them to see that even if, up to this point, they have done the best they could, there might be the possibility to do more in the future. It is not helpful, particularly in this beginning stage, to behave as a neutral, impersonal observer or commentator. This makes them more anxious and perhaps confused. Be an active participant and reveal your desire to help. You facilitate their sharing openly and honestly and motivate them toward increased reflection and introspection.

There are times, especially when starting work, that clients need direction and structure during interviews. Begin at the surface. Gradually proceed into greater depth, step by step. Clients expect that you give ample attention to their presenting problem or complaint. Try not to get totally caught up in it. Understand the immediate concern that brings them and allow it to direct your learning who they are. When you devote almost exclusive attention to the "problem," you compromise the "person." Clients expect, indeed need, you to consider them as people with problems, not the reverse.

Let them know that they will be doing most of the talking. Let them know that things sometimes seem to get worse before they get better. It takes time for a problem to develop, and more time for it to be remedied. Remind them that their range of choices is greater in the present than it was in the past. Let them know that their range of choices in the future will be that much greater as they come to terms with themselves and their history. Let them know, therefore, that you might explore their past with them in order to expand present and future choices.

Notice and build on what they do well. Enable them to recognize that they can be their own best resource. Proceed cautiously from the outside, from the skin, to the inside, toward the viscera, as does a skilled surgeon. In so doing you not only show caring, but learn a great deal about clients from witnessing their adaptation and integration — all displayed in the way they present themselves and behave in relation to this new situation with you.

Clients perceive you as possessing special skills and abilities, as planful in your actions. They may also distort you in a variety of ways — see you as a lover, an ally against a hostile world, or a miracle worker. You are obliged, at some level, to accept the status and authority with which they invest you while creating mechanisms for correcting distorted images. Because expectations are a central force in stimulating behavior, be alert to what is expected and how you assimilate this into your conduct.

Double-check that you provide a sense of direction without being restrictive. Stimulate and guide without bias and pressure. Be conscious always of the ultimate purpose of meeting clients' needs. Convey a sense of hope. You can do this by making explicit to clients the way in which information they provide will be used, what is expected of them, and what they can expect. For example, explain how the financial data that they are reluctant to offer may enable you to obtain health services they require but cannot afford. Honestly note exceptions to confidentiality. When it is necessary to confer with your supervisor about specific concerns posed by clients, inform them of this course of action and identify the selected details you intend to share. These are some fundamental ways of letting clients know that you are with them and that you are available to assist them in making new discoveries about themselves and their situation.

HOW TO APPROACH THE INITIAL PHASE

During your first and early contacts with clients, you will see them under stress. They probably will displace feelings from other relationships and situations onto you and this contact. Recognizing this about them can be very illuminating. Their basic characteristics and patterns will be manifested, indeed exaggerated. Because of this, you will have a sharper portrayal of them. This clearer image, taken in concert with whatever content clients relay in words about themselves and their problems, enhances your ability to:

— Understand how clients see themselves in relation to their problems
— Identify precipitants for seeking help
— Specify attempts at resolution
— Evaluate internal stresses
— Define external pressures
— **Assess and correct expectations**
— Break global issues into smaller problems
— Formulate preliminary goals

—Establish limits
—Ascertain commitment and motivation
—Establish ground rules and procedures
—Glean clues to major themes
—Estimate obstacles to progress.

You are attempting to achieve a comprehensive overview of the behavioral, affective, and cognitive characteristics of your client. Since you must move ahead very often on the basis of limited knowledge, structure is essential to set a climate conducive to observation and interaction. You translate the general purpose of the interview into a series of specific objectives or requirements that affect the range, depth and transitions of the exchange. Although the interaction is reciprocal, your influence on the client is greater than the client's influence on you. Figure 2 seeks to capture the spiral process of proceeding during these first contacts.

Continually ask clients to help you understand what is troubling them and what is happening to them as you interact. Let them know what information you already have and its sources and get their reaction to it. Pace and lead the discussion. If you can, convert questions into statements; if you must ask questions, break big questions into smaller ones and, when possible, leave the questions open-ended. Make yours an inquiry, not an interrogation. Avoid feeding clients the answers you want them to give. Try not to bury the answer you expect within the body of your question. Be sure to request "feedback" by paraphrasing and restating what you hear clients say. Ask for their comment, giving them a chance to correct your understanding or repeat what they mean. As you develop ideas or hypotheses about clients, check them out directly. Ensure that you and your clients are aware that you are going somewhere.

SOME HINTS FOR BEGINNINGS

There is no formula for effective help giving because it is a dynamic and organic process, not a static entity. While there is no standardized format to follow, you need to have in mind some definite ideas, some considerations about how to initiate and maintain the flow.

FIGURE 2

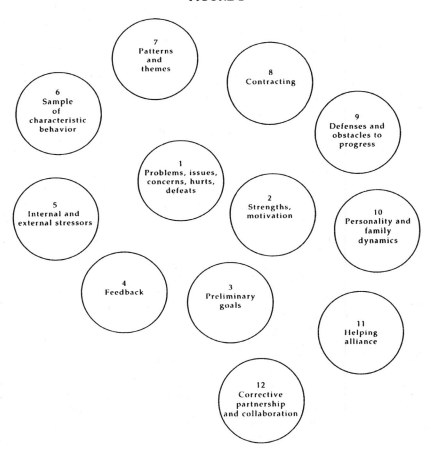

It is especially important to strike a balance in these first contacts between being too much or not enough help. "Size things up" so that you do not interfere where you are not needed.

— Be curious, not nosey, to stimulate wonder.
— Be definite, not rigid, to enhance self-determination.
— Be caring, not sloppy or sentimental, to sustain trust.
— Be compassionate, not judgmental, to open communication.
— Be collaborative, not authoritative, to build bridges.

— Be respectful, not paternalistic, to enhance esteem.
— Use ordinary words, not jargon; they clarify perception.
— Be candid, not oblique, to encourage participation and direction.
— Explain all along what you are doing, to foster cooperation and continuity.
— Respond to feelings, not only to ideas, to provide relief.
— Be creative, not complacent, to free imagination.
— Be daring, not safe, to offer challenges.
— Be readily accessible to reduce irritation and suspicion.

Explain along the way what you are doing and why you are doing it. For example, preface questions with the remark, "I'm going to ask you a question about . . ." combining it with an explanation of why you want the information. Use language that matches and reflects that of your client. Exercise clients' drive and capacity to face themselves and their situation more fully, competently, and independently. Enable clients to explore their own life spaces because of your presence, not despite it. Recognize and reinforce progress, and reflect specifically on success. Provide opportunity to practice new behaviors. Give guidance and direction without pressure. Do not hesitate to offer sound advice; no one ever suffered from good advice. When selectively suggested and not imposed, advice can stimulate thinking and decision making. There may be times when it is helpful to say simply, "At this point, just forgive yourself. You may have erred in the past, but you are unlikely to behave that way again."

Sequentially order your interventions. They are absorbed more fully when progressively built upon. Strengthen linkage with others. You may not always be the best available helper. State honestly when you cannot help or do not know how to proceed.

Increasing client autonomy results from reciprocity in your transactions. You should both have responsibilities. How these are distributed has to do with the goals toward which you are working, clients' capacities, the conditions under which they live and under which you work, and the dynamics of this particular relationship.

Be sensitive to sequence and progression, and timing. Observe and respect clients' "space" and "style." What you convey by doing so is that you find what they say and how they say it meaningful and that you want to hear more. What you say is, "I have time for you and I care about you."

Adjust your methods of working to meet clients' needs, personality and style. This is the premier professional stance. Clients should not be expected to adapt to one particular method of help-giving; rather, you should have the knowledge, skill and experience to find the most effective approach to help them.

WHERE DO I GO FROM HERE?

Toward the end of initial interviews, summarize the session. Consolidate gains. Recapitulate what has transpired. Explain the next steps. Ask clients if they have any specific questions that you can help with now. Your clients have been vulnerable and are probably raw at this moment. Walking out into the real world again might seem frightening. They may feel that they have given part of themselves away. Soothe the rough spots. Give them something to take away. This may be something as palpable as an appointment card or a handshake, or as intangible as a compassionate glance. It is important for clients to leave with something from you which conveys understanding and belief that change is possible. This sustains them. Assign homework, reading, or other activities and make sure that your next interview time is scheduled.

Tell them what will happen next and that you are willing and available to them.

A CHECKLIST TO GUIDE YOU IN ASSESSING FIRST CONTACTS

Following is a checklist to consider in relation to yourself, your clients and the process of interaction during the initial stage of help-giving.

Preparing:

_____ Unclutter your mind and direct thoughts only to your client
_____ Clear your desk and office

_____ Create a warm "space"
_____ Collect notes, lists, and papers, and have them accessible
_____ Minimize the chance of interruptions
_____ Reserve this time exclusively for your client
_____ Anticipate specific questions or concerns
_____ Review available information
_____ Initiate the dialogue
_____ Suspend your biases
_____ Walk a mile in your client's shoes

Setting the stage:

_____ Greet the client cordially
_____ Use words that convey welcome and intent to help
_____ Use gestures to demonstrate interest and attentiveness
_____ Use gentle and frequent eye contact
_____ Lean forward
_____ Show that you are listening by nodding and smiling
_____ Inquire rather than interrogate
_____ Note themes and patterns
_____ Focus on what the client says and conveys
_____ Do not put words into the client's mouth
_____ Do not use canned responses
_____ Reflect back to the client what you hear him or her say
_____ Listen to the client's reactions to your feedback
_____ Check the accuracy of your understanding

Enabling participation:

_____ Start at the surface and gradually work inward
_____ Explain your need for information
_____ Explain your role and the client's
_____ Be selective in your questioning styles and types
_____ Be clear and concise, and avoid jargon
_____ Approach exchanges from several points of view
_____ Be aware of your own nonverbal behavior
_____ Structure the interview
_____ Repeat important information
_____ Ascertain client's strengths

_____ Be generous with support and guidance
_____ Convert questions into statements
_____ Customize your style to your client's

Closing:

_____ Reach for clear, open agreement with the client
_____ Clarify what is likely to happen
_____ Pull things together
_____ Ask your client to recap the interview
_____ Ask if there is something else you ought to know
_____ Use polite gestures in closing
_____ Plan next steps
_____ Schedule another appointment
_____ Explain how the process is to proceed

If you were to do it over again, what would you change? What would you keep the same? What did you learn about yourself from this contact?

REFERENCE

Frost, Robert. *Collected Poems of Robert Frost*. NY: Henry Holt & Co., 1930.

Chapter III

Creating a "Safehouse"

Competent therapists fluctuate between the limits of a scientific discipline and the infinite possibilities of inspired intuition.

—W. Robert Beavers

Psychoanalysis is in essence a cure through love.

—Freud, in a letter to Jung

Spy and detective novels, movies and television shows have made popular the notion of the "safehouse," a completely secure location where inhabitants are free from danger. In novels such as those by Ludlum, Higgins and Le Carre, safehouses are places to take shelter from pursuing enemies for a short time.

Safehouses are not merely a romanticized fictional notion. They do exist in fact. As far back as biblical times, "the six cities of refuge" provided security for those who unintentionally killed another person. In the middle ages, Abelard established a safehouse, "The Paraclete," where he found sanctuary from those conspiring against him. Today police and justice departments provide safehouses for key witnesses threatened because of their testimony in criminal cases. Adversary nations maintain temporary hideaways in hostile territories to safeguard their agents. While these locations are supposed to be secret, eventually they are found out. But an unwritten code requires that once in the door, the agent remains immune from pursuit.

The safehouse is a palpable and powerful metaphor for the helping process, clarifying and unifying such diverse characterizations of the helping process as gratification and abstinence, neutrality and anonymity, the real and the transferred relationship. Clients require an anchorage. Here they can literally and figuratively escape for a time from dreadful thrashings. They can find refuge from the dangers and hurts of the external world and from accompanying internal fears. In a safe harbor, they can find calm. They can patch their tears. Just as in novels, the safehouse for clients provides a respite from painful events and trauma compounded by internal injury. Its climate is warm and accepting.

But respite is not enough. Trauma takes on a private symbolic significance for clients, who interpret trauma according to their own internal psychic realities. In the safehouse of the therapist's office, clients not only experience relief from their anxieties but come to understand, meet, and overcome their sense of brokenness. Your office offers a "holding space," in Winnicott's phrase, for accepting clients' feelings and affirming their strengths. Away from a barrage of abuse, criticism, neglect, and rejection, they can be free to move deeper into themselves.

The important things to recognize with regard to the safehouse is that it is not a return to symbiosis but is a place of structure and transition where communication with you gives clients a growing ability to find themselves.

Because clients come to you at a time when their usual adaptive defenses are weakened, your safe retreat helps them to reinstate familiar and healthy defenses. Here they learn certain strategies to come to terms with this present trauma as well as some dynamics of their internal life that may have made them vulnerable to being overwhelmed or too depleted to find solutions. Success depends upon their revising their view of themselves, others and the world. The safehouse is where you counteract their expectation that they will inevitably fail, that others will be uncaring, and that they will be left to struggle alone. In an atmosphere of positive expectancy and support, clients are restored and better prepared with new skills for returning to face a world that is at times dangerous and violent. In returning, however, because they have been rejuvenated and have discovered previously untapped resources, they are even better able to brave the stress and strain of living.

In the safehouse you supply some of the nurturance which was originally missing from clients' lives. The safehouse is a sanctuary, not unlike the one described by Winnicott (1986), as necessary for "good enough" mothering, that which is needed in the present to allow the realization of full potential in the future. In this close, rather than distant, association of warmth, rather than coolness, clients can consolidate themselves. The "good enough" mother is your model for the therapeutic situation. Some children experience being held, cradled, cuddled and protected from dangerous objects and harmful experiences. Others grow up in an unsafe atmosphere of abuse. Yours is to offer another experience of renewal to those clients who originally experienced it, restoring their balance, and to offer it for the first time to those who never experienced it. In either case, "holding," accepting, and respecting them impels them deeper into themselves so that they learn to "hold" themselves. Eventually they gain insight into themselves because while you nurture, you also interpret their condition.

In the safehouse, clients are not forced to rely solely upon their own already depleted resources. They do not have to "make do" with their lacks and limitations. New possibilities are provided. A temporary shelter where they can find peace and balance in a world askew, the safehouse offers a place where change can take place, a space where clients can disarm themselves and lay aside their fearfulness. The painful past can be revealed, unremembered hurts can be reexperienced or experienced as an adult for the first time. Through remembered emotions, a search can be undertaken for a better future.

For some clients, like Ms. Wall, a better future does not even seem like a remote possibility.

Ms. Wall, a 26-year-old single parent of three children, one of them handicapped, had lived in a single room of a welfare hotel in the inner city of a large metropolitan area until they were evicted. She continually abused drugs even while enrolled in a drug treatment program. While there was considerable evidence of child abuse, this situation had never been addressed. Occupying a cardboard "shack" on the sidewalk of a large conference center, panhandling, struggling to keep her family together and still dealing with her drug habit, she agreed to move into a shelter, to make life easier.

The shelter provided a room, a set of rules to follow, and a caseworker who capitalized on Ms. Wall's desire — reluctant though it was — to be clean and sober. Concentrating first on providing food, shelter, clothing and medical treatment, along with drug rehabilitation, Ms. Wall was encouraged to connect with other women in the facility who supported and encouraged her to "stick with the program." The shelter's stable, structured and predictable environment, and the worker's persistent attentiveness, contrasted greatly with the disrupted, uprooted and abusive home that she had known as a child.

Active caring, combined with limit setting and information and proficiency skills needed to care for her children, in a way she herself had not been cared for, improved her parenting behavior, and engendered a sense of mastery and esteem. This change did not occur without the worker first tolerating Ms. Wall's initial hostile verbal assaults, and then helping her to examine them as part of her troubled pattern of relating to others. Exploration increased her understanding of the adverse results her self-destructive behaviors — drug abuse, angry outbursts, and manipulations — caused her.

Establishing the connection between her actions and her feelings when she engaged in self-defeating behavior, released painful feelings and helped her to recognize that such behavior was often a defense against further possible physical and emotional injury. Reflecting on feedback about her own negative attitudes and patterns, Ms. Wall became more consistently self-soothing and self-reliant in her behavior toward herself and her children.

The shelter, marred by torn flooring, graffitied walls, musty odors, but furnished by Ms. Wall with her own pictures and decorative plants, became not a palace, but a place of pride.

In the safehouse of your relationship, clients, as Ms. Wall, pass through a metaphoric version of developmental maturation. They depend on you for their well-being. This is akin to the developmental process through which we all journey on our way from absolute dependence to autonomy. Recapitulated in the safehouse with you is a version of the infant's complete reliance on caretakers. As time passes, the child develops his own way, and caretakers have the task of permitting individuality to emerge and separation to take place. This is a multi-stage process. So it is with your clients in the safehouse.

At first, attention is paid to provision of staples necessary for survival and vigor. Focus is then directed toward connection and communication. The third step involves regulating the self, freeing repressed needs and learning new methods for self-support. Clients learn new ways of thinking and problem solving and come to self-knowledge through the facilitative conditions and interpretations you provide. Knowledge and insight, of course, must be translated into actual change in daily life, through repeated practice to refine change.

Ultimately, clients become sufficiently whole and consolidated to build a more permanent, personal, inner "safehouse" for themselves so they can leave your temporary safehouse to venture out on their own with a lasting sense of being at home with themselves.

Make your office a secure base where clients can take

> temporary refuge from the demands and distractions of daily life . . . He can participate in complex, emotionally charged rituals, suspend his critical faculties, freely express his emotions, indulge in leisurely self-exploration, daydream, or do whatever else the therapy prescribes, secure in the knowledge that no harm will come to him during the session and that he will not be held accountable in his daily life for whatever he says or does during it. (Frank, *Persuasion and Healing*, 325)

A VIEW OF HOME

A profound way of understanding what clients require to get back on course is getting a glimpse of their first home. Although their description of "home" may relate to the past, you will learn from it about what constitutes their internal paradigm for present issues of trust, safety, entrapment, hiding, exposure. In reflecting on and talking about their home, clients present a telescopic view of the significant places and people who fashioned their history. Asking them to draw a floor plan of the home where they grew up, for example, sparks memories and feelings about family, friends and events. Their simple narrative about home demonstrates the complex relationship between their living space and the nature of their inner lives. Clients create their environments while the environment affects how they live. Their description of "home" provides for you a mirror reflecting the world from which they came as well as their inner vision of it which continues to hold them. The soft and cozy nests, the unassailable castles and the womblike closets they build and inhabit provide you with an organizing metaphor, capturing not only a picture of their original home, an image of their inner life, but also a guide for establishing the form of your safehouse. During the course of your work, changes in their "home" indicate changes within their perspectives and within themselves.

Carol: Finding "Home"

The following case illustration demonstrates how one client's view of home influenced the focus and direction of the helping process. Carol's metaphor for her background and for herself was the absence of any "safe place" in her life. Establishing a safehouse made it possible for her to overcome multiple present and past trauma and to find meaning within her current interactions with the world.

Carol, a 28-year-old graduate nurse, had been seeing me for approximately eight months when she was violently brutalized, raped, and sodomized in her own apartment. Crawling to her telephone a few hours later after she regained consciousness, she called the police who took her to a local hospital. She undressed and waited over one hour for the attending physician, only to be summarily discharged without examination. The hospital had no rape kit. Taken to yet another hospital, she undressed again for the third time that evening. Unable to reach friends or family, she returned home alone. She had no safe place — now or ever, so it seemed. Even the safety of being inside her own body was ended. She was broken into, violated.

Away at a conference, I received a frantic call from Carol. She was desperate. She did not know where to turn. In contacting a rape hotline, as was recommended by hospital staff and police, she had been counseled not to continue to work with me, a man. Such advice added to her confusion: it further paralyzed her. She had always felt secure with me and stable in our work; but now, frazzled, she was getting upsetting advice that contradicted her own instincts. Could she trust me? Could she trust anyone? Could she trust her own instincts? Was there anyplace where she was safe from harm? Compounding her sense of helplessness, isolation and despair was the fact that her friends, apparently not knowing how to comfort her, were avoiding her. Shunned by them at the time of her greatest need, she was shamed and devastated; indeed, she started to blame herself for her suffering.

Carol was reassured over the phone by my open caring and concern. We sifted for a few hours through the events that occurred, her reactions to them, and the choices available to her. She decided to continue working with me. She also decided to start attending a special group dealing with rape victims. Immediately upon my returning from the conference, our work resumed.

Carol had come originally seeking help after a series of disastrous relationships with men. She was also extremely dissatisfied with her job, her profession, and herself. Early in our work, it became clear that Carol's historical and inner "home" was troubled. She grew up in an alcoholic household where she was the oldest of four children and the only female. Her mother worked, frequently leaving Carol to care for everyone else and for the house which was literally crumbling around them all. She was repeatedly abused physically and berated verbally by her father. Her three brothers continually taunted her. She felt abandoned by her mother. Her recollection of her home and the people in it was grim and sad. She came to believe that men were inevitably cruel and disappointing. She refused to follow in her mother's footsteps, finding her disorganized and unavailable. She recalled her home being violent and in shambles, an armed camp or a hovel. This image of Carol's home, while certainly relevant in our beginning work, became paramount, along with the rape, as a focal point for reflection, an available and vivid symbol of all her dilemmas about family and self.

Carol had deliberately set up her own apartment to be totally different from her parents' house. It was peaceful, ordered, clean and free from threats. She designed her home to be a sanctuary, not a prison. After the rape, her home had become a fortress, not a castle. The meaning of this central metaphor, representing her past and present state, was continually elaborated and explored.

Our work together was structured to provide an atmosphere of validation and emotional sharing. Feeling "at home" as our work progressed, she found release in catharsis, and support in cognitive interpretation and restructuring of her central metaphor of "no safe place." This structure helped contain and control what she experienced as her inner chaos.

Significant breakthroughs were promoted by Carol's ongoing use of a log, in the form of index cards, on which she recorded memories of the incident, an incident that intensified repressed residual feelings of failure, defeat and emptiness from her past. On these 5 × 8 cards she also recorded her dreams, dreams in which she continually relived the pain and humiliation of the rape, but in which she also revealed the emotional process of gradually coming to grips with it. As these cards were sorted, re-sorted and examined, the story of the rape incident, and its accompanying metaphor, acquired a central role in her deeper deliberations about herself and her family.

All this material led to increasing associations and affective connections. Carol gradually filled the gaps in her understanding not only of the rape, which had precipitated such intensive exploration, but of more buried and previously inscrutable markings in her life. As she did so, she came to fathom the deeper sources of her pervasive feelings of unimportance, worthlessness and powerlessness, to make connections to her earlier experiences of deprivation and neglect over which she had no control. She came to recognize that she did not provoke and was not to blame for all that she had suffered. She was able to take control of the events, herself, and the situation.

Carol came, finally, to remember that she did not simply submit to her attacker. She had struggled against him at knifepoint. This discovery resulted in her being able to muster energy and perseverance to press charges against her assailant and to testify against him in court, even though it involved rehashing the details of the trauma. She had gained mastery over it and felt sufficiently strong and revitalized that she asked her father to join her in a few sessions with me to clear the air about the rape, for he had treated her as disgraced, perhaps blameful, and to address and seek to resolve the long-hidden issues between them.

Carol did not want to conclude the work, which extended over a period of three years. She wanted to cling to what was safe and sure; however, she recognized that she had found and could rely upon the safe place within herself.

In the safehouse Carol came to acknowledge the horror of her rape and the horror of her background, but, replenished, she came back to face and to participate in it. Not withdrawing and finding a "safe place" within herself, she learned to utilize it as a resource to draw on in reestablishing an identity and a personal meaning system. Carol currently has a new apartment, is gainfully employed, and is dating.

Relinquishing the Safehouse

The safehouse is simultaneously timeless and temporary. It is timeless because it does more than merely remove stress or symptoms. It involves a shift in the client's experiential world. It serves as the model and instrument for clients locating within themselves a safehouse to which they can continually turn for succor and growth. The safehouse is temporary insofar as clients cannot stay forever. Ultimately, no caretaking is permanent. Clearly, something must happen in the safehouse for clients to leave it. If they remain, their circumstances would become as unbearable as those they fled. The safehouse would become a prison. Just as a nursing mother must wean her baby or stifle its growth, so you must encourage your clients to separate when they are ready. Their readiness is determined by the degree to which they are ready to tolerate separation and have achieved mastery of internal emotions. Separation can bring freedom and exhilaration as attachment can sustain growth. Paradoxically, healthy detachment requires attachment.

ATTACHMENT BEHAVIOR AND EMPATHY

The safehouse is a metaphorical way of conveying what the professional literature refers to as attachment behavior, the holding environment, and empathy.

Attachment Behavior

Attachment behavior is viewed by Bowlby (1975) as any form of behavior resulting in an individual attaining or retaining closeness to another differentiated or preferred individual, usually conceived as stronger or wiser. While it begins early in life, attachment behavior continues to be apparent throughout life, especially when a person is sick, upset, or frightened. It is characterized by (1) specificity and long duration, (2) emotional arousal, (3) a critical period for its development, (4) appearance even in the face of punishment, (5) maintaining proximity to the attachment figure as a "secure base," (6) reciprocal behavior by the attachment figure, (7) functioning to protect the individual from danger (Bowlby, 292). When there is confidence in the availability of attachment figures (when, in other words, you are available to clients), they are less prone to either intense or chronic fear. Put simply, they need to count on you in time of need for mutual understanding, giving support, valuing them, and promoting their well-being. Your safehouse is the place where clients' inherent capacities for hope and faith, deadened by misfortunes and horrors in the present and in their original home, can be restored.

Empathy and the Holding Environment

The technical name for your attunement to clients in creating a safehouse is "empathy." There is a strong parallel between being a parent and being a professional helper. You do not need to be perfect, but you do need to be good and sensitive enough to your clients' needs to accept and go along with their positive and negative struggles. It is, indeed, re-parenting. This is no small order. How is it possible to enter your client's world to such an extent that you can actually alter the way that he or she perceives and subsequently deals with the world? Empathic listening and understanding form the basis of any effective intervention (Kohut, 1984). We do not make an instantaneous leap of enlightenment but rather engage in a multifaceted process. We show the capacity to project ourselves (while remaining separate) into the inner experience of another.

There is some debate about what empathy is, how important it is, and how it works. Confusion abounds about its definition and significance. This can be expected, for empathy is defined differently by different philosophies and theoretical orientations. Results of research studies based in these theories are certainly not illuminating. It is not fully clear what part empathy plays in producing positive therapeutic outcomes. Questions arise. Is empathy rational or irrational? Does it involve only affect, or cognition as well? Is it only cognition? Is it a mode of observation, or is it projection? Is it a form of identification in which a temporary loss of self occurs? Is it conscious or unconscious? Is it a capacity, a trait, a process, or a form of communication? Is it predictive? Situational? Is it verbal, non-verbal? Neither? Both? Is it experience distant or experience near? Is it the same as sympathy? As love? Does it heal? It should be no surprise that such a complicated phenomenon defies easy explanation.

Regardless of its complexity, "empathy" is commonly used to refer to your ability to come to know first-hand, so to speak, the experience of your clients. It is considered a necessary, but not sufficient, condition for the helping process. Basch (1983) points out that Freud considered empathy to be indispensable when it came to taking a position regarding another's mental life. The father of psychoanalysis viewed empathy as the process playing the largest part in our understanding of what is inherently foreign to our ego in others. Rogers (1958) sees empathy as including both cognitive and affective elements. Cognitive empathy refers to intellectually taking the role or perspective of the client. It means seeing the world as the client does. Affective empathy refers to responding with the same emotion to the client's emotion. It means feeling the same way as the client does. Rogers also emphasized the need for the helper to communicate this understanding.

Psychoanalytic writers identify the more subtle aspects of empathy. For example, Greenson (1967, 368-9) stated that

> empathy means to share, to experience the feelings of another human being. One partakes of the quality of the feelings and not the quantity . . . It is essentially a preconscious phenomenon; it can be consciously instigated or interrupted; and it can occur silently and automatically oscillating with other forms of relating to people.

Kohut (1977) explains empathy as a basic human capacity which not only operates as a therapeutic tool but also defines the field of our observations and interactions by letting us know that there is an inner life. He refers to empathy as "vicarious introspection," and argues that empathy can only be understood empathically. He explains that a clinician "uses his sensory impressions, of course . . . but these sensory data would remain meaningless were it not for his ability to recognize complex psychological configurations that only empathy, *the human echo to human experience*, can provide" (1978, 700, emphasis mine). Kohut postulates that the empathic responsiveness of the helper participates in the repair of developmental empathic failures caused by unempathic parents (1977). Empathy, then, is both exploratory and explanatory.

As I have mentioned earlier, Winnicott (1986), too, emphasizes the theme that good helping is good mothering. He argues further that "good enough" mothering is more a matter of who mothers *are* than what they do. One element is providing a setting for trust where the significant variable is the "interpersonal relationship in all its rich and complex human colours" (Winnicott, 1986). He refers to it as "care-cure" which is essential for every human being and which *"can only become fact in each individual case because of good-enough mothering"* (Winnicott, 1986). He believes that in many cases what clients need is a "good enough mother" or "bad" helper or really just a human being who in the process of making "mistakes" allows clients to reexperience traumas in an adult way for the first time.

Barrett-Lennard describes the process of empathy as a multistage sequence where

> empathy is first and foremost an inner experience, a responsive experiential resonation in keeping with the responding person's set to be this way. For such an empathic inner response to have an impact on the other—which is another, distinct issue—it must of course be expressed or made visible in some way to that other. And when it is expressed, its effect will necessarily depend on qualities of the receiver as well as on the signal of the sender. (Barrett-Lennard, 93)

Hogan, in studying empathy, substantially agreed on the characteristics of a highly empathic person. These characteristics include (1) skill in imaginative play, pretending, and humor; (2) awareness of the impression one makes on others; (3) ability to evaluate others' motives; (4) insight into one's own motives and behavior, and (5) social perception.

Empathy, then, involves a personal capacity, affective resonance and cognitive understanding. All are operative and complementarily interwoven in interpersonal functioning. Fosshage (1981) suggests that we are capable of two different modes of mental activity: One visual and sensory with intense affective colorations serving overall integrative and synthetic functions; the other conceptual and logical, making use of linguistic symbols serving an integrative and synthetic function. These modes of mentation may be described as different by complementary modes of apprehending, responding to, and organizing the external and internal world. He emphasizes that despite specialization of function, both hemispheres of the brain process not independently, but complementarily. The degree to which each is utilized in the helping process varies from client to client and from situation to situation.

There is sufficient theoretical clarity and research evidence across the disciplines to indicate that empathy is multi-faceted. It is a trait, an emotional and cognitive capacity which can be activated and a state manifested in thoughts, feelings or behavior and demonstrated in a multi-stage interpersonal process. It involves cognitive understanding of another combined with affective resonance. Both exploratory and explanatory, it comprises vicarious feelings and associations, coupled with correct understanding.

Put in less theoretical terms, empathy is a spontaneous and temporary experience occurring within you, the helper, having affective and cognitive components whereby you come to know and comprehend what clients mights be experiencing. It is a mode of gathering information about clients' internal worlds by attending to your own experience in the presence of clients. It requires an ability to oscillate from observer to participant and back to observer. It is important because it allows you access to clients' inner experience, and in doing so, moves you away from any tendency to objectify clients and view them simply as the repository of symptoms or problems. It also dampens any tendency to treat them as bad, devouring or manipulative. It is an essential prerequisite for your ability to "be empathic" — to voice your understanding of clients in such a way that they feel understood and soothed. This feeling of being understood and soothed provides a connectedness that diminishes clients' feelings of aloneness and alienation, and thus strengthens your working alliance with them.

Empathy has the potential to bring the clarity of rational logic to bear upon the profundity of affective experience, a way to synthesize two apparently antithetical figures: the dispassionate and rational scientist and the attuned resonating artist.

Providing a safehouse, then, can be considered as metaphoric shorthand for being empathic.

HOW TO BUILD A SAFEHOUSE

You start to build a safehouse for clients by making yourself accessible to them; you actively offer your assistance in helping them design their plan for change, not as a passive participant but rather as an active collaborator. You do not simply observe your clients but enter into their experience on a fundamental level to get to know parts of them that they may not know. A critical component of drawing the blueprint involves being aware of what you bring into the process yourself: that you influence the design. It also involves knowing the strength, shape, texture of the materials with which you will be working so that they can be employed to maximum advantage.

Digging the cellar and laying the foundation involve getting information that is buried and supports the structure. In the unending relationship between our needs, wants, and wishes and environmental demands and restrictions, we learn ways to react and form patterns which make it easier to adjust to the environment. Some of these patterns are functional and others are not. Identifying them requires immersion into clients' inner lives and experiences; it involves repetitive interactions that sometimes get boring but create shapes, so that old patterns are uncovered and the possibility for creating and altering new ones is enhanced.

You may have to abandon the customary approach of neutrality and aloofness. Enter the experience with them. It is interesting to note that therapist/clients seek in their own therapeutic work a personal relationship, one in which they feel affirmed, appreciated, and respected by another human being whom they like, appreciate, and respect (Grunebaum, 1983). *Harmful* treatment experiences result from a rigid, distant and uninvolved interaction. Be highly visible as a facilitator of communication and have a capacity to contain and catalyze behavior and emotions that are denied, projected, and acted out by clients. Providing a containing safehouse is a prerequisite for effective work and serves as a basis for change. It has been suggested that you have become a helper partly in search of a safehouse of your own. Providing a safehouse for your clients serves you as well.

Your role is that of a host who welcomes clients. Be consistent and available. Be generous, receptive and responsive. Show appreciation and patience. Create an ambiance of trust and support. Face clients squarely. Show that you are present to them. Make your own reactions available for them to study. Impassivity cheats you and clients of your most useful instrument — your own experience and ability to see and to share.

You can make a difference if you are receptive and remember to:

— Delight in the endless variety and unexplored mystery of people;
— Be curious, take risks, and be open to challenges;
— Experiment, innovate, be original and creative;
— Rely on both artistic intuition and scientific intellect;
— Know that you do not have total comprehension;

— Be humble, vulnerable, and open to discovery;
— Be a nondistorting mirror reflecting clients' unknown aspects;
— Recognize that your power is based on your ability to face your own inner reality and face it responsibly;
— Take time; do not rush to get instant results;
— Have the courage to admit your mistakes and failures;
— Change what you're doing when it doesn't work;
— Trust and pursue your imagination; daydream;
— Endeavor sincerely to get in touch with clients;
— Discover your own blind spots and free yourself from excessive anxiety and coldness;
— Be generous and kindly.

Building a safehouse does not mean fusing with your clients. This would be as destructive as a lack of compassion or understanding. It means, rather, opening a dialogue where clients are expected to help you understand them, rather than your showing superior wisdom. In a safehouse there is activity as well as reflection, doing as well as saying, extrospection as well as introspection. Emphasis is placed on the human experience of an active, striving, affirming and potentiating transaction, on recognizing the continuity of the "there-and-then" of the distant past with the "here-and-now" of the immediate present. Both, taken together, establish the conditions for change. The novelty of such integration serves as a catalyst for growth.

If you cannot get yourself into the client's shoes and somehow give them relief as well as resources, the work will dissolve. Have your actions match your words. Clients will progress when they experience your "holding" in an intense way. Kohut writes: "I must now, unfortunately, add, that empathy per se, the mere presence of empathy, has also a beneficial, in a broad sense, a therapeutic effect—both in the clinical setting and in human life, in general." (1982, 85). Why "unfortunately?" Kohut feared that such a direct statement would expose him to the suspicion of abandoning scientific sobriety and of entering the land of mysticism or sentimentality. He wanted to maintain his objectivity. But he was on target.

The safehouse is more than a symbolic dwelling. It is as much a holding environment for you as it is for clients. When you involve yourself and participate fully with clients, your experiential learning will match theirs.

REFERENCES

Barrett-Lennard, G. "The Empathy Cycle: Refinement of a Nuclear Concept," *Journal of Counseling Psychology*, 28 (2), 1981.

Basch, Michael. "Affect and the Analyst," *Psychoanalytic Inquiry*, 3 (4), 1983.

Basch, Michael. "Empathic Understanding: A Review of the Concept and Some Theoretical Considerations," *Journal of the American Psychoanalytic Association*, 31 (1), 1983.

Bowlby, John. "Attachment Theory, Separation Anxiety, and Mourning," in *American Handbook of Psychiatry*. 2nd e., Vol.VI, D. Hamburg & H. Brodie, Eds. NY: Basic, 1975.

Fosshage, James. "The Psychological Function of Dreams." Paper presented at Long Island Association of Psychoanalytic Psychologists, Long Island, NY, 1981.

Frank, Jerome. *Persuasion and Healing*. Baltimore: Johns Hopkins University Press, 1973.

Frank, Jerome. *Psychotherapy and the Human Predicament*. NY: Schocken Books, 1978.

Greenson, R. *The Technique and Practice of Psychoanalysis* Vol. 1. NY: International Universities Press, 1967.

Grunebaum, H. "A Study of Therapists' Choice of a Therapist," *American Journal of Psychiatry*, 140, 1983.

Kohut, Heinz, *How Does Analysis Cure?* Chicago: University of Chicago Press, 1984.

Kohut, Heinz, "Introspection, Empathy, and the Semi-circle of Mental Health," *International Journal of Psychoanalysis*, 63, 1982.

Kohut, Heinz, *The Restoration of the Self*. NY: International Universities Press, 1977.

Kohut, Heinz, *The Search of the Self*. NY: International Universities Press, 1978.

Rogers, Carl. "The Characteristics of a Helping Relationship," *Personnel and Guidance Journal*, 37 (1), 1958.

Winnicott, D.W. *Holding and Interpretation*. NY: Grove Press, 1986.

Winnicott, D.W. *Home is Where We Start From*. NY: Norton and Co., 1986.

Chapter IV

Contracting Through Goal Setting

If you have no goals you have nothing to reach for.

— Farmer's Almanac

The illusion that one can unilaterally control other people underlies many problems that bring clients to therapy. My dilemma as a therapist is how to free people from this illusion without buying into it myself.

— Lynn Hoffman

The helping process should be one of mutual influence between clients and you. A contract based upon goals provides you with a powerful helping tool for proceeding in this direction. Incorporated directly into the helping process, goal-oriented contracting promotes genuine collaboration in exploring needs and identifying goals. It goes beyond "tell me what to do" to mobilize the resources of clients in self-directed activity, and enlists their cooperation in identifying and determining to a significant degree the shape of the helping process. Furthermore, goal-oriented contracting provides a concrete and objective means for measuring and documenting progress and growth.

Following are the three most significant characteristics of contracting:

1. Contracting demands active participation of both clients and you in the helping process. When you work together to identify goals, participate in achieving them, and help shape the direction of your work together, it is difficult to remain detached from the process.

2. Contracting bridges the gulf between clients and you; it creates a sense of empowerment. There is often a sharp distinction between

those who deliver service and those who receive it. It is doubtful whether this sharp distinction benefits either party in the helping process. It is more likely that it impedes progress. When you collaborate with clients, the power line is crossed and they can assume responsibility for themselves in a fundamental way.

3. Contracting means that change is an interactive endeavor, not a process where you "pour" answers into clients as if they were receptacles to be filled. Contracting encourages clients to see their task as making change for themselves and their lives; at the same time, it encourages you to see yourself as creating avenues for change.

COLLABORATIVE CONTRACTS

Contracts structure intervention around observable, measurable and mutually acceptable goals which clients themselves state in terms of favorable outcomes. Contracting emphasizes clients' active part in finding their own solutions. When clients are fully involved in outlining the direction of the process, you are more likely to avoid any possibility of inadvertently maintaining or exacerbating their problems. Contracting provides a step-by-step account of how clients think and feel; it also offers a sample of their typical behavior patterns. Such information helps both of you to work in tandem to tackle problems.

A contract is an agreement between clients, the consumers of service, and you, the provider. It specifies purpose, issues, goals and objectives, procedures and constraints, roles, and time for your work together. Such a dynamic tool reduces anxiety, provides clarity of direction, and verifies success since clients are maximally involved at every juncture in defining and examining their own needs, problems and strengths. They are, subsequently, more ready to participate in the process because every effort is made to start where clients are. Involving them fully reduces resistance and motivates them to participate in the change effort.

This chapter presents a model of contracting and gives practical answers to frequently asked questions about contracting: What kind of information should be included in the contract? How can it be used in a systematic way throughout the helping process? Can contracts be modified? Should it be written? What are its disadvantages as well as advantages? Are there times when contracts are counter-indicated? and How does a contract affect client expectations?

BASIC ASSUMPTIONS ABOUT CLIENTS, GOALS AND CONTRACTING

Goals

Goals provide a common ground for your joint venture; they:

— Ensure that both of you agree about what is to be achieved
— Provide direction for the helping process and prevent aimless wandering
— Foster clients' self-determination and self-directed activity
— Facilitate collaboration in selecting appropriate strategies for intervention
— Assist clients and you to monitor and document progress
— Promote focus on what realistically can be changed
— Open avenues of communication and
— Correct distorted perceptions.

An anagram summarizes the function of goals:

"G" alvanize work by generating graphic guidelines gauging the work
"O" perate on an orientation to observable outcomes organized around options and objectives
"A" ttend to action and achievement
"L" aunch and lead work through the leverage of listing and labeling
"S" tructure the corrective situation by selecting strategies, skills and sequence of intervention (Fox).

Clients

Undergirding this approach is an optimistic and positivistic view that clients:

1. Can and should make informed choices
2. Know much about themselves which can be stated in easily understandable terms
3. Can share in the responsibility for the helping endeavor
4. Have the capacity to consider and evaluate the accuracy of their needs and wants which can be expressed in the form of goals
5. Know how much they are willing to invest in the therapeutic endeavor and can articulate this
6. Already possess strengths and capacities that can be enlisted and extended in the helping process.

Clients know much about what ails them and have valid ideas about resolution. Rather than limiting attention to problems, contracting builds upon clients' available strengths and resources so that the helping process becomes construction rather than simply repair or restoration.

Contracting

Contracting is a philosophy of intervention relying on clients' cooperation in designing the helping process. It emphasizes participation and involvement in a deliberate, genuine, and voluntary partnership with you where mutual assessment and exploration about common grounds for action are encouraged. Creating a contract facilitates communication and activates commitment to the difficult process of change. Open acknowledgment of and respect for clients' input fosters autonomy and self-determination; it also reduces any sense of helplessness by providing some level of control over what happens in your work together. An atmosphere of acceptance and involvement promotes flexibility in the therapeutic endeavor. Clients lead the work: they do not have to fit into your preconceived notion of helping. The process is tailored to clients' expressed and unique needs and special concerns (Fox).

Contracts take different forms — preliminary contracts which establish the parameters of the relationship at the initial stage as it acquires focus and purpose; primary working contracts which are formal agreements about goals, procedures and responsibilities; and mini-contracts which focus on particular tasks or special needs within the framework of the guiding contract. With each new client I see, I propose a preliminary 8-10 week contract to enable both of us to determine if the work "fits." During this time clients not only have the opportunity to experience how I work, but I have the opportunity to observe firsthand how they function. In addition to regularly scheduled face-to-face interviews, clients are asked to complete an inventory, described fully in Chapter IX, and to keep a log, described in Chapter X. Experiencing this preliminary "test" contract, each of us, now having sampled what ongoing work might involve, can more knowledgeably and freely decide whether or not and how to proceed. Sometimes, no further contact is needed because the preliminary contract resolves the problems presented. More frequently, the preliminary contract paves the way to a primary contract; the R family contract described in detail later in this chapter is an example of a primary contract.

The usefulness of a mini-contract is illustrated by work with John. John, a 44-year-old recovering alcoholic, who had during eleven months of intensive work at a men's shelter, moved from "skid row" to his "own place," was warned that his chain smoking was hazardous to his heart and lungs. He had considerable difficulty in quitting, continually reverting to approaches that did not work — exercising "willpower," going "cold turkey" and puffing on cigarette substitutes. We devised a mini-contract to stop smoking, within the context of the established primary contract, to meet John's acute and special need.

Carrying around a small piece of paper in the cellophane of his cigarette pack, John recorded the frequency, specific times, circumstances of "lighting-up" and feelings that accompanied this ritual. The exaggerated attention paid to lighting-up, coupled with the task of writing, spotlighted for John striking aspects of his behavior of which he was unaware. More importantly, guided by our discussions, he began to recognize specific types of anxiety that smoking relieved and realized that these were associated to his former drinking binges. Concomitantly, he obtained positive reinforcement for his achievement by graphing, at my suggestion, the frequency of smoking when he started this regimen and its decline over time. The effect was cumulative and improvement was progressive because change was visual and could be attributed to his own efforts. Smoking ceased. John also came to better understand sources of and responses to his anxiety which continued as the focus in our primary contract.

Whatever form contracts take — preliminary, primary or mini, they draw upon the same principles alliteratively stated that

Contracting is a
Central concern for both clients and clinicians; it promotes
Cooperation, fostering
Choice and Collaboration about
Concrete and Concisely stated behavioral goals and
Considers Consequences of Change in a
Consistent Climate which encourages
Compromise,
Clarity, and
Commitment to
Common goals.

A bonus of contracting in any form is that its various procedures, detailed later, are themselves guidelines for clients to follow in their day-to-day problem solving. When coupled with close attention to the current life context and to rehearsal, clients are able to transfer new skills learned in your office to real life situations. The process of contracting also educates clients about what it is reasonable to expect from the entire helping process.

Keep in mind that contracts are not chiseled in stone; they are open to alteration and renegotiation. They can and should be revised whenever emergencies arise, new data are presented, or contingencies of the immediate situation require it.

WHY GOALS?

By positively stating concerns in terms of favorable outcomes and by emphasizing a desired state, goals propel your work with clients in a positive direction. Goals are not simply a vehicle for assessment but are an integral part of the total intervention process and provide criteria against which to measure progress and performance. Clients reasonably wonder, "Are your goals the same as mine?" and "Are you confident we jointly will be able to achieve them?" Getting affirmative answers to these questions, through observing the very way you interact with them, motivates them to proceed.

Setting goals is not a static or isolated activity; neither is it one restricted to the helping process. It is a necessary and recurring process faced daily by clients. Goal setting within the helping process is a natural and felicitous activity because it transfers directly to day-to-day life by focusing attention on achieving desired states rather than on eliminating negative conditions.

Goal setting is ego enhancing because clients realize that what they think and feel is taken seriously as an integral part of the helping process. They set the foundation for the work. When you place demands on clients, believing that they are capable of fulfilling them, you create hopeful expectations. Remember, the greater the importance of the goals and the greater the expectation of achieving them, the more likely clients will act in ways to attain them (Fox). Sometimes achieving goals is sufficient reward for clients. It is possible, however, to add incentives directly into the contract for accomplishing named tasks.

The benefit of establishing what the "end" should look like at the outset of the helping process is that it defines and directs present interaction. Highlighting possibilities rather than problems accelerate change because strengths are mobilized and barriers anticipated before they occur. Explicit, observable and measurable, goals provide tangible evidence of accomplishment. Since results of helping are often elusive and hard to define, goals, as they are achieved, afford a sense of gratification, furnishing an identifiable marker of success.

There are three types of goals—final, facilitative, and functional.

Final goals are statements of "ends," of terminal conditions or results, naming what is hoped ultimately to be achieved — for example, "Harry will stop physically beating Lowella," "Carmen will move out of the shelter into public housing," "Seth will get better grades in school and be promoted," "The foster family will adopt Maria."

Facilitative goals are statements of "means," of action and/or incremental steps, stepping stones, describing how the ends are to be accomplished including both clients' and your activities — for example, "Harry will be taught how to express demands and argue using words," "The worker will accompany Carmen to prospective apartments," "A twice-weekly tutoring program in math at the agency has begun," "Forms are being completed jointly by the Judds and worker."

Functional goals are statements of operating arrangements, conditions and ground rules for involvement including time, place, duration and participation — "Weekly, one-hour counseling sessions are scheduled," "Carmen will phone housing projects to set up visits for herself and worker," "Worker will confer with Seth's teachers every second week," "The paperwork must be completed within two months."

Optimum use of goal setting occurs when goal setting is guided by the ten steps illustrated in Figure 3.

Goals should be specific, making a concrete, definite, and precise statement of intent in simple, understandable language. Explicate the goals; do not assume that clients understand fully what you have agreed upon until you both openly and directly restate the goals. If you sense some reluctance or discomfort in discussing a particular portion of the contract, take it as a cue to spend more time assisting clients to more plainly state what they want.

Goals need to be feasible particularly in regard to clients' capacities. They should also be realistic and attainable in terms of whatever time is available. The goals, methods, roles and tasks set forth in the contract should be within your or the client's reach. Do not promise more than you can deliver and do not expect from clients more than they can give. Be sure that clients do not agree to actions which they cannot carry out.

A major purpose of the contract is to keep clients moving at a

FIGURE 3. Ten Steps in Goal Formulation

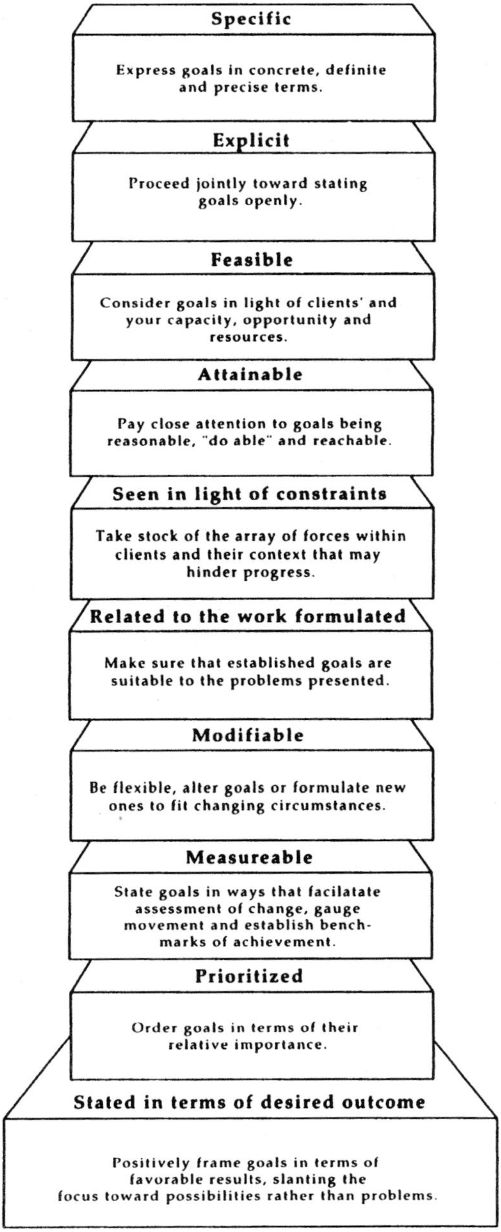

Specific

Express goals in concrete, definite and precise terms.

Explicit

Proceed jointly toward stating goals openly.

Feasible

Consider goals in light of clients' and your capacity, opportunity and resources.

Attainable

Pay close attention to goals being reasonable, "do able" and reachable.

Seen in light of constraints

Take stock of the array of forces within clients and their context that may hinder progress.

Related to the work formulated

Make sure that established goals are suitable to the problems presented.

Modifiable

Be flexible, alter goals or formulate new ones to fit changing circumstances.

Measureable

State goals in ways that facilatate assessment of change, gauge movement and establish bench-marks of achievement.

Prioritized

Order goals in terms of their relative importance.

Stated in terms of desired outcome

Positively frame goals in terms of favorable results, slanting the focus toward possibilities rather than problems.

steady pace, not to shame or punish breaches. Not all contracts go smoothly. When there are significant differences between you and your clients, work them out early. Do not avoid conflict. When contracting goes too smoothly, it is often a sign that one side is selling out to the other; furthermore, an agreement between worker and client not to pursue service because of recognized differences or conflict is, in fact, a good contract (Seabury).

PROCEDURE FOR CONTRACTING

Your ability to find and respond to patterns in clients' behavior rests on the adequacy of your methods; in other words, the kind of answers you get are limited to the kinds of questions you ask. Although, in the end, the effort to change must come from clients, you have a key role in assisting them in shaping change through identifying clear goals.

In the initial phase of work, jointly examine and assess clients' initial expectations, capacities, and goals. Identify, at the same time, your own areas of expertise in terms of approach and resources. When needs and goals are explicated and agreed upon, confusion diminishes about the direction and content of the work (Fox). The following questions guide your matching the unique needs of clients with the requirements of the therapeutic task:

1. What specifically needs to be done?
2. On what do we agree?
3. What is required?
4. What do we expect from each other?
5. Who will do what?
6. In what sequence?
7. What constraints exist?
8. How will we know when we have achieved it? (Fox)

Answering these questions jointly not only moves clients and you toward establishing a genuinely reciprocal and collaborative relationship, but builds a clear-cut and firm foundation for change. Work is clearly defined and steps are delineated for corrective measures. Concentrate at first on the most important issues to the client, but, over time, feel freer to spread efforts over the range of concerns clients may introduce during the course of work.

Goals can be developed for change in thoughts and feelings as well as in behavior. Whichever the focus, the very process of systematically attending to goals moves clients away from irrational and self-limiting thinking about themselves, others, or their situation. Clients also come to recognize what cannot be changed. When goal setting, specify an end result for each goal.

Contracting usually occurs in four stages —

1. Selection of goals
2. Delineation of what is to be changed
3. Planning action
4. Feedback for evaluation.

The first stage involves clarifying competencies — clients' and your own. It also sets communication and collaborative arrangements. Mutual determination of purpose and limits leads to mutual investment and commitment. The second phase involves the actual collection and analysis of data, identification of range of options and decisions needed, and consideration of alternatives. The third stage actually mobilizes you and your clients toward establishing a workable structure. The final stage balances the goals with the plan of action so that ongoing correction and modification can be made as you move forward achieving the identified results.

OUTLINE FOR THE GOAL-ORIENTED CONTRACT

Below you will find an outline for the goal-oriented contract. While for illustrative purposes it traces an actual contract with a family, the process and procedure are equally applicable to work with individuals or groups. Its eight points are not discrete entities and usually overlap. The outline exemplifies an actual *written* contract with the R family employing the actual language and style of the family. The family consisted of four members: Mr. R, a 38-year-old draftsman; Mrs. R, a 36-year-old part-time nurse's aide; John, their 12-year-old intellectually gifted son; and Sally, their 9-year-old daughter. The R's had come for family therapy as a last resort after a series of unsuccessful attempts at individual work for John. John, having a superior I.Q., was not achieving his potential in school. Indeed, he was not attending school at all much of the time. His sister Sally, an average student, was a model student and daughter. For purposes of clear illustration this example traces only one of five goals the family identified, namely, to improve the relationship between Mr. R and his 12-year-old son, John. Other goals included: to improve school performance measured by more frequent attendance and completion of homework; to reduce Mrs. R's over-involvement with John and Sally measured by her transporting them less to all activities by car and hiring a babysitter when she shopped or ate out rather than always bringing them along; to develop a better relationship between Mr. and Mrs. R in terms of their spending more time alone, increasing the frequency and duration of sexual relations and building on common intellectual and sporting interests.

1. Clients and you generate baseline information. This is contextual data describing clients, their situation, their needs and concerns as the work begins. It enables clients and you to capture a "before" picture of the initial level of functioning against which change "after" the contract can be measured. The baseline information addresses the question, "What is the original level of functioning?" An example statement from the actual contract with the R family reads, "Mr. R and John spend little "good" time alone together. The only time they relate is when Mr. R punishes John for not doing his homework. Mr. R wanted John to play baseball and signed him up for the Little League, but never goes to watch the games. All he does is criticize John for what he doesn't do right."

2. Clients and you then specify your focus and expectations. You discuss explicitly what you want ultimately to achieve and record it. I use newsprint and keep goals posted at all meetings. At the same time, identify proximate and incremental goals. These are stated in concrete terms so it will be possible to know when they have been achieved. This procedure helps determine what kind of approach is necessary and narrows down possible strategies while discovering additional information. It answers the question, "What is to be accomplished?" A statement of expectation from the actual contract was, "Mr. R and John agree that they want to like each other better

and spend time together in an enjoyable way. They agree that for one month Mr. R would relinquish the responsibility of John's homework to John. Mr. R will take John to one baseball practice and one baseball game each week. As a fresh start, they will together begin the tree house that John has wanted and Mr. R has promised to help him build.''

3. Clients and you proceed to set priorities for goals. Goals, after being considered in relation to their feasibility and clarity, and after being stated in a terse fashion, are ordered in terms of their importance. The question guiding this part of the contract is, ''What is the relative importance of each goal?'' Attention is directed at the central or most important one first. The R family agreed that the ''awful'' relationship between Mr. R and John was the most pressing issue and needed immediate attention.

4. After establishing the conditions to be changed, clients and you identify observable behavioral characteristics, and describe how changes will be exhibited by them. This segment of the contract is crucial since it establishes a tangible sign of achievement for clients and you. It answers the question, ''How will improvement be recognized?'' The actual contract statement read as follows: ''For one month Mr. R and John will spend at least four hours each week with each other. Mr. R will note how much time they spend together without arguing. John will keep a record of how many homework assignments he completes each week, Mr. R will note each time he was tempted to criticize John's homework, baseball or building skill but refrains.''

5. Clients and you delineate your respective roles and explain your responsibilities. Here you elaborate on the requirements for participation, by each of you answering the question, ''What are we willing to offer?'' For example, ''Mr. R and John are willing to carve out six hours to spend with each other each week in selected activity. They each will keep records suggested by Dr. F, and will honestly report weekly results. Dr. F will read the reports, continue to coach and offer suggestions and work out a reward system with Mr. R and John.''

6. Clients and you develop a plan which includes alternative solutions. You devise a method for review of the work. The guiding question for this portion of the contract is, ''What is the most effec-

tive way to tackle the problem?'' A sample statement from the contract is, "It's good to gradually stop some of the negative criticism. More important is doing some new 'good' things together. The progress will be examined week to week but also more thoroughly after the first month."

7. Clients and you agree on a time frame. Included are such factors as duration of the contract, length of sessions, and progression sequence. The guideline questions are: "How much time will it take to achieve the goals?" "How much time must be put into preparation?" "How much time will be devoted to each meeting and to each task?" and "In what sequence will the contract be implemented?" The actual contract read, "For the first goal we will put aside one month, meeting each week for 1 1/2 hours. Time outside the session devoted to this goal will be six hours as described earlier in the contract."

8. Clients and you build-in and specify criteria for step-by-step evaluation of the achievement of goals and transferability into actual life at home. The method for the measurement of change is agreed upon with the question being, "How will progress be measured?" or "How will achievement be demonstrated?" For example, "by the end of one month John will be doing his homework alone each night; Mr. R will be attending practices and games without criticizing and the tree house will be half completed . . .''

PROGRESSIVE STEPS
IN THE CONTRACTING PROCESS

When developing contracts, be sure that

— the problem is clearly defined
— the goals are spelled out
— the work that needs doing is delineated
— the alternatives are considered
— the work is organized into clear jobs
— the tasks are related to each other
— decisions are made about sequence, method, etc.
— feedback is elicited

— progress is evaluated

— necessary revisions and alterations are made.

WRITTEN OR ORAL CONTRACTS

There is always an implicit contract between you and the client when you start working. Written contracts, however, are better than oral ones because they reduce ambiguity and avoid misunderstanding. If it is not written, it should be thoroughly verbalized and discussed. A written contract is an immediate and tangible reminder of agreements that conceptualizes problems, gives form to the chaotic nature of initial requests, and also provides a visual document that makes it possible to get easily back on track when resistance or obstacles have led you astray. Neither "written in stone" nor as binding as a legal document, the "spirit" of the contract, mutuality, is most important.

When I work with clients I record and revise the wording on newsprint as goals are stated and changed. This newsprint, posted at every session, serves as our written contract. As each goal is achieved, it is crossed out, accentuating success; as new goals are identified, they are listed. My clients' participation and cooperation is continually enlisted in the development of the contract. Not as inflexible as it may sound, the contract does not preclude but rather encourages you to deal more spontaneously with crisis and other pressing issues that invariably arise during the course of the work; structure frees you for spontaneous interaction.

BARRIERS TO CONTRACTING

There are several roadblocks to effective contracting. To begin with, excessive attention to problems delimits involvement. Attend rather to clients' strengths — these must be enlisted anyway to grapple with problems. Too, when clients look for some concrete help for specific problems, and you look for major personality change through introspective techniques, impasses and conflict are bound to occur, opening the way to disappointment on both sides, and, often premature termination. If agreement is too easily reached, it may mean that someone is holding back or attempting to avoid confrontation for fear that the conflict will be unresolvable and work will terminate. Very likely, attempts to avoid conflict eventually lead to unresolvable differences later on. Other barriers include unrecognized fears, rigid behaviors and persistent thought patterns that defend clients from facing change. In families and couples, deeply entrenched dysfunctional patterns of interaction, which protect them from facing themselves and which preserve the status quo, forestall contracting. What can you do about these powerful blocks to change?

Take account of what *can* be accomplished. Avoid doing too much for the client both in terms of formulating the contract and in carrying out its tasks. By doing too much "for" clients, you support their own beliefs that they are inadequate and unable to plan or care for themselves. It may be quicker and easier to do it for clients, but, in the end, it is more helpful to encourage them to take responsibility themselves. Know when to step back and allow clients to take increasingly active roles. Let them know (and remember yourself) that the contract is one aspect of a larger helping process. Do not ignore issues as they arise during the course of your contact. Restricting your attention only to what has been agreed upon originally is a mistake. Also, use precise language to identify what is to be changed, to determine goals you are working toward, and to evaluate progress.

ADVANTAGES AND LIMITATIONS OF CONTRACTING

Goal-oriented contracting takes three important principles of growth into consideration: clients progress most effectively when they see a need, know how and are involved.

The exchange between the clients and you during contracting involves the dimension of mutual decision making and agreement. In coming to look at and formulate a plan, you together develop a viable system which defines and nurtures the helping process.

Advantages

A major feature of goal-oriented contracting is that it introduces genuine collaboration into the helping process. It is fluid. It makes possible individualized work and mobilizes ingenuity and energy to perform tasks. The contract has many other advantages. Explicit, it is a source of motivation and of involvement. Time-limited, it eliminates a protracted and indefinite time frame. The limit is established in direct relation to the requirements of the client needs.

Contracting promotes focus and avoids ambiguity by clearly explicating problems and goals. It avoids games and hidden agenda that frequently accompany the helping process and thereby minimizes control and manipulation. Commitment to carry it out is enhanced. Stating goals clearly at the beginning gives guidance and direction to both clients and you and sets criteria for evaluating the undertaking. Initial success, symbolized by the very existence of a contract, gives impetus for continued expectation of resolution and confidence that continuing effort will lead to success and positive results.

A seldom-mentioned issue is your need to see that you make a difference, that you make an impact on clients' problems. Goal-oriented contracting allows for such gratification because it provides you with tangible signs that something is being accomplished (Fox).

The advantages of goal-oriented contracting in terms of assessment, treatment and evaluation are described below.

Assessment

The goal-oriented contract permits earlier, quicker and more accurate assessment. Directly observing clients undertake the process of identifying goals in the session illuminates how they characteristically interact in their home environment. It provides data immediately about roles, hidden bonds, and strengths which may not be otherwise available. As the client is observed undergoing self-reflection and analysis, knowledge is gained about existing capacity for reality testing and flexibility in adaptation. Precision in identifying themes and issues is enhanced and any impact of intervention is seen immediately. Clients' capacity for reality appraisal, flexibility in dealing with tasks, and altering patterns becomes evident as does their unique emotional, cultural, and social context.

Process

The contract encourages precision in describing and designing interventive methods for resolution thus keeping you and clients more attuned to the stated purpose and conduct of the work. Tension is relieved because abstract global concerns are broken down into manageable concrete terms and logical frames. Immediate modification of dysfunctional communication patterns and support for productive ones are an added advantage of contracting. Distorted perceptions are corrected and mutual exchange and examination are encouraged.

Because goal setting is central to the entire helping endeavor, contracting complements and facilitates, rather than intrudes. New avenues of communication are opened and unhealthy patterns are explicated as clients observe themselves involved in planning change in their lives through mutual exploration and compromise. Immediate feedback about how the work is progressing allows for modification.

Even when clients are involuntary ones, see no problems, or have reduced capacity to abstract or visualize outcomes, goal-oriented contracting is possible because it invites them to choose an outcome they desire. Clients are more inclined to "own" what they have designed and not see it as imposed, and therefore oppose or rail against it.

Evaluation

As is clear from the contracts with John and the R family, presented above, the goal-oriented contract provides systematic data about the effect of intervention for clinicians, but more importantly, for clients. Comparing initial and subsequent statements on the contract, or any portion of it, provides tangible evidence of progress. Contracting makes evaluation possible, indeed easy, because it employs a practical methodology which integrates criteria for single system research into the clinical procedure: specifying problems; measuring them; collecting information about them over time, both before and during intervention; using a planned format or design and specifying an intervention program (Blythe and Briar).

DISADVANTAGES OF CONTRACTING

Despite its many advantages, there are some limitations to contracting. In the first place, it may be seen as oversimplifying a very complex process. Because contracting is a relatively formal process, it may be viewed as static and binding. The contract is not intended to be rigidly or blindly followed; rather, its very intention is to promote flexibility. Problems occur when it is inappropriately used to address routine matters that are by definition not negotiable. For example, a limitation arises from misperception of the contract. It is not a cure-all. It is not a prescription. It cannot do more than enable clients and you to deal with a few well-defined and circumscribed issues which are capable of being worked on within a defined time frame. Finally, it is limited by reality. The contract is only as good as the people who formulate it. It cannot be expected to accomplish more than the resources, expertise and investment that clients and you bring to it.

Goal-oriented contracting can be described as much by what it is not as by what it is. Not intended for particular types of clients, a compromise or a substitute for other types of work, or a device to be employed to be expedient, it is a deliberate and effective treatment of choice for a gamut of client situations. Its use is not limited to certain practice agencies or fields of practice. It has relevance for all types of human services: mental health, child welfare, and medical.

A FINAL NOTE ABOUT CONTRACTING

Goal-oriented contracting structures intervention around observable, measurable and mutually acceptable goals. This chapter describes the rationale, principles and procedures for undertaking such an approach. It is illustrated with a case example illustrating a family contract. Goal-oriented contracting encourages individuals and families to function independently, making more possible the transfer of change from the therapeutic situation to real life. It is based on the operational principle of "starting where the client is."

It is an approach which demonstrates to clients the relationship between their interaction and the problem; it examines and then establishes and reinforces appropriate vehicles for client development, growth and stability. It makes it possible to adapt the helping process to different types of clients. It teaches clients to observe their own process and establish new and better modes of communication and support, and encourages higher levels of differentiation.

I believe that contracting intrinsically contains the possibilities for confronting the fullest and deepest range of your clients' experiences. Clients come initially to work on identified "symptoms" or problems. These are genuine problems for which they ought to receive help. Once in the helping situation, as clients formulate the contract and begin to work on the problem, the depth, breadth and quality of your presence, sensibility, and courage encourages them to fathom, ever more completely, the fullness of their life story.

REFERENCES

Blythe, Betty and Briar, Scott. "Developing Empirically Based Models of Practice," *Social Work*, November/December, 1985.

Fox, Raymond. "Short-term Goal-Oriented Family Therapy," *Social Casework*, 68 (8), October, 1987.

Seabury, Brett. "Negotiating Sound Contracts with Clients," *Public Welfare*, 37 (2), 1979.

Chapter V

The Helping Relationship

Behold, I do not give lectures or a little charity, When I give, I give myself.

—*Walt Whitman*

The overtones are lost, and what is left are conversations which, in their poverty, cannot hide the lack of real contact. We glide past each other. But why? Why—? We reach out towards the other. In vain—because we have never dared to give ourselves.

—*Dag Hammarskjold*

No man is an island. No client, no family, no group, no therapist is an island. We are defined and continually influenced by relationships. The core of our humanity is that we live our lives in relation to other people. Relationship is the essence of our existence.

From our earliest hours of life we are formed and form ourselves on the basis of our experiences with others. Who we are is the result of these interactions. Current studies of personality development identify relationships as the dynamic core which makes us human (Mahler, Litz, Cameron, Goldstein). Elements of each relationship and the ability to accept or reject a relationship contribute to who we are. Without relationships we cease to exist. Babies who are not held and nurtured soon die—often physically, always emotionally. In short, we are creatures who throughout our lives require contact and connection with others.

And so it is true for clients seeking help.

It is within the context of the helping relationship that clients' perceptual distortions, maladaptive behaviors and paradigms about self, others, and the world not only come under challenge, but are changed. Within the context of the helping relationship, both clients and you deal either explicitly or implicitly with: (1) past experiences that have affected your ability to relate to others; (2) the *here and now* experience of the physical, emotional and perceptual state of your transaction; and (3) each of your expectations of the other and the process.

Can anything more be said about the helping relationship? The answer is yes. No form of help can succeed unless you first convince clients that you understand them and are concerned for their welfare.

We tend increasingly in the helping professions to be pragmatists. What we like to see is efficiency. What is harder to see is caring, the instrument of change and development. Caring is more elusive, ambiguous, harder to quantify. It requires our participation in pain and our sharing in the experience of suffering. When we continually attempt to refine our understanding of caring in relationship, we are in a better position to offer consolation and hope. Caring does not mean falling into a sentimental trap; rather, it means establishing a vehicle of concern which cultivates the field of intellectual curiosity and exploration. Caring alone cannot resolve problems. However, being cared for gives clients the courage to talk honestly and directly about their troublesome lives.

We tend to run away from painful realities or to try to change them quickly. But cure without care makes us manipulators in the most negative sense and prevents a quality of "betweenness" that exists when two people are truly present for each other. In this view, you are an active participant in an affective as well as cognitive reciprocal interaction with clients, an interaction in which you both come to understanding and "change" over the course of time. Be ready, willing, and eager to dive into deeper waters even though clients may pull back in terror from such exploration. The very way you attend to them, "be where they are," reduces their fear of facing uncertainty and furthers an ongoing personal dialogue which expresses, shapes, and enriches your immediate experience together. As a consequence, clients are less inclined to slip back into maladaptive functioning.

THE DEVELOPMENT OF THE HELPING RELATIONSHIP

The therapeutic relationship develops in a way similar to other interpersonal relationships. From the initial attraction between clients and you in the initial meeting, and from your mutually negotiating contract arrangements, communication opens both to produce further interaction and to enhance cohesion. The relationship is the keystone for the practical, personal, and theoretical elements of your professional helping. When clients feel understood by you, have confidence in you, and contribute to how the work proceeds, positive outcomes result.

The impact of helping resides in how well you use yourself and your sensitivity to guide clients' journeys in understanding themselves. The most important vehicle available to make this happen is your ability in the relationship to model behavior, reflect attitude, and explore thinking and feeling. Change can thus be understood as a process by which clients begin to experience themselves in different ways, so that their previous self-experience and experience of others becomes untenable.

Put yourself in your clients' shoes. The process of helping demands that you understand how clients view the world. Empathic understanding means more than mere knowledge of how clients feel. It means the capacity to actually feel what they feel. For clients, having you understand what it is like to be them encourages different ways of experiencing. Clients' attachment to you, combined with your empathic resonance, provides an anchor allowing them to weather emotional storms and a mainstay to fathom uncharted waters. This corrective experience that allows clients to experience themselves differently, and thereby make changes, is a function of the extent to which you can, leaving any preconceived notions aside, get inside them, be where they are, and share their world.

The essence of successful helping is clients' achieving trust in you as a therapeutic instrument. If this cannot be realized, the outcome of the helping process will be thwarted. If it can, stability, identity, and awareness are achieved.

THEORIES OF THE HELPING RELATIONSHIP

The professional literature speaks of relationship as the vehicle through which help occurs. It emphasizes core conditions in the relationship necessary to inspire change. Rogers described these as: genuineness—your ability to know yourself so as to be fully present to your client while remaining truly yourself; accurate empathic understanding—your ability to enter the feeling world of the client; and unconditional positive regard—your trust in the process of growth and self-actualization.

Strupp identified core relationship conditions as respect, interest, understanding, tact, maturity and firm belief in the ability to help. Compton and Galaway conceptualized them as concern for the other, commitment and obligation, acceptance and expectation, empathy, authority and power, and genuineness and congruence. Frank described these as: learning—instillation of new cognitions; hope—enhancement of positive expectancies; mastery—provision of success experiences; sharing—relief of alienation through human contact and arousal and, emotional, not merely intellectual, stimulation.

In conducting an extensive review of psychotherapy-outcome studies, Gurman came to the conclusion that warmth, liking and acceptance are significant contributors to client's rating of outcome (Grunebaum). Other research supports the centrality of these aspects by highlighting what is harmful in the therapeutic process. Part of how we undertand what is helpful is to understand what is harmful so as to avoid it. Helpers characterized as distant, cold, unengaged and lacking in "human quality" were seen as harmful. You can probably add being indifferent, demanding, guilt provoking, judgmental, and dogmatic to the list.

Marziali and Alexander, in their review of the research literature of the past decade, demonstrate the relevance of the therapeutic relationship for predicting positive outcome in diverse models of therapy. They assert that the relationship is a potent curative factor in all forms of treatment.

The optimum relationship is characterized by one or more of the following: warmth, acceptance, respect, understanding, closeness, interest, maturity, and trust. Your aim is not simply to recapitulate, and then supply what was originally missing or repair what was faulty in clients' lives, but, rather, you create an atmosphere of responsiveness, expectancy, and hope where new perspectives are possible. You bring, in other words, empathic capacity as well as scientific understanding to your exchange.

Identifying characteristics of the helping relationship as discrete entities is misleading and somewhat artificial because they are so interwoven. Ways of describing one component of the relationship are often the same used to describe another. More importantly, it is unlikely that you will develop a relationship by focusing on any one relationship characteristic and deciding, for example, "I will be 'accepting.'" Relationship is not built in that way. Relationship is synergetic and includes all the elements mentioned above, in dynamic interdependence. It is more and greater than all its parts.

By way of summary, relationship signifies *agape*, in Greek, the highest form of love:

AGAPE

A — Acceptance
G — Genuineness
A — Actuality
P — Positive regard and
E — Empathy

Clients absorb and identify with your delicate and immediate facility for emotional exchange and your comfort with such sensitive matters as dependence, conflict and power. Through the relationship, you help clients more fully understand and effectively use their personality strengths to overcome dysfunctional patterns. You accomplish this by providing an *in vivo* experience of empathic resonance with them. You offer a firsthand sense of the rich depth of the human mind, an appreciation of the strength of inner or intrapsychic forces, and a grasp of the power of human contact.

Helping is not always positive. There are some attempts that fail. Clients' uncertainty about themselves, others, and the world can be so powerful that it can have negative consequences. The quality of the experience with you, however, is key to facilitating commitment and change. Figure 4 reprints an article published in *The New*

York Times by a social worker who worked with homeless children. I include it because it captures the spirit of a caring relationship.

FIGURE 4

I Tell Homeless Kids, "Love You, Baby"

*The following is adapted from "Voices from the Street," a play about homeless people written by them and those who work with them in Washington. This excerpt was written by a social worker.**

By Ella McCall

For me, 600 of the most endangered children in the world are the 600 children who live in the shelter where I'm a social worker.

How can I convert a motel on a screeching thoroughfare into a sanctuary where a family can find peace from the war that poverty has waged against them? How do I help people to survive in one crowded motel room when up to seven people have to share space that would drive one person stir crazy?

How do I help devastated babies and mothers and fathers feel like greeting each new day with a hopeful heart? How do I repair broken hearts and shattered dreams?

These are challenges for which my education and experience as a social worker never prepared me. Even though I'm the mother of seven children and my oldest is an adult, I still dream of what I really want to be when I grow up.

In a family shelter, there isn't even the luxury of space for private tears. I don't have a magic wand to cure depression in a child. I can only say, "Love you, baby" and pray that the family will find normal housing before it's too late for that baby.

I don't have a magic wand to help the mothers of these children who have lost everything from their former homes to their self-respect. To see your baby in pain when you can't make the pain go away is a terrible curse for a mother to bear.

I don't have a magic wand to keep the jackals of the drug world from addicting my mothers. I don't have a magic wand to make my little babies fall out of love with fancy sneakers, designer clothes and the seduction of toys advertised on TV. So when the jackal with his drugs goes knocking on the desperate doors of my 7, 9 and 10-year-old babies and says, "When you take this stuff, you're gonna feel like Christmas every day," how long can these children resist the temptation? I

*The play "Voices from the Street" was written in coordination with Suzanne C. Goldman.

need nothing less than an army of God's avenging angels to keep these babies safe from harm.

I've got no magic wand to make my babies want to go to school. These innocent little ones are ashamed of their address:"I'm hurting real bad, Ms. Call, I wish I weren't alive." In their schools where peer approval is the kiss of life and peer disapproval is the kiss of death, the other kids call them "dirty baby," punching them with their fists and their words.

My babies are just as smart and beautiful and good as other babies. They've survived times that would try the soul of the strongest man and they're just little kids.

Those who have not tasted the tears of my babies say, "Ella, you love those babies too much!" The thieves of poverty, deprivation and drugs have already robbed them of a happy childhood. How can I rob them of my hugs? How can I deny them my kisses?

Yeah, I know, I've flunked "professional detachment." I think that I'll never learn professional detachment. You see I was a mother myself when I was 14. I'm the mother of seven children. I was raped, abused, on welfare and homeless, just like the people I serve. When I could find no light at the end of the tunnel, good folks with unconditional kindness said, "Love you, Ella."

"Love you, Ella" gave me the push to get my high school equivalency diploma. "Love you, Ella" gave me the courage to earn my bachelor's degree from American University. "Love you, Ella" gave me the self-belief to get my master's degree from Catholic University.

You can never say "love you" too much. My job as a human being is to say "I love you" until my last breath. There are hundreds of thousands of precious and irreplaceable resources in homeless shelters across this land. They are as endangered as any wilderness park, any river, any rare animal in America. When together we can say "Love you, baby," together we will begin to save our babies.□

SELF-AWARENESS

A constant challenge you face is separating your personal from professional roles and responses. This is an especially difficult endeavor because helping denotes by its very nature an interrelationship between your life and your work. Yet you are required to make a productive separation.

It has been emphasized that only when you are alert to who you are and what you are doing are you sufficiently relaxed, clear, and open-minded to understand the client. In other words, it is impossible to be tuned into the feelings of others without first being attuned to your own. For example, Helen, who was from a poor family and raised in a low income housing project, had serious trouble working with middle-class clients. She could not fathom why they stopped seeing her shortly after the first interview. She never verbally disparaged them, but tacitly dismissed the problems of economically "better off" clients as being insignificant.

Your personality, values, and sensitivity are the very tools which make you an effective therapeutic instrument. They determine what happens in your interaction with clients.

Your own past and present conflicts may interpose themselves on your functioning with clients. They may urge here and restrain there. They may hinder the effective work as they compel and censor behavior. They may diminish and distort experience and perception governing what you selectively perceive. Mark, like many helpers before him, was the oldest child of alcoholic parents and the one charged — precipitously and prematurely — with raising three younger sisters. As a helper, he constantly found himself "overinvolved" with clients — rescuing them, doing everything for them, not allowing them to undertake the simplest tasks for themselves. His own background had left him unable to trust that anything would be done if he did not do it; that things would ever work out if he did not take charge; that he had value beneath and beyond his caretaking role. As he came to see himself in a new light, his effectiveness as a helper increased.

Unless you know what is going on within yourself, it is tempting to blame clients for a feeling of being stuck. When you come to acknowledge and monitor your own process of denying, distorting, or projecting, when you recognize your inner stirrings, then these processes may, in fact, be called upon as resources to enhance your work.

To be helpful to others, you must understand, rein, and resolve your own conflicts and problems so that they do not interfere with your ability to understand others'. The loathing that Winetta, a compulsive clinician, inevitably felt for anyone who was late, emotionally detached her from clients and undermined her relating to them on any other basis than their lateness. The capacity "to perceive one's behavior as objectively as possible, to have free access to one's own feelings without guilt, embarrassment, or discomfort, is a necessary, if not sufficient, prerequisite for the controlled subjectivity the helping process demands" (Kadushin, 152).

You face a difficult charge. You are expected to be responsive to clients without letting your own feelings intrude or interfere. You are required to draw upon them in the service of clients as a guide to understanding and intervention. This is a delicate balance. Since you can react only from what is within yourself, you must know yourself so that your capacity for being in relationship is increased, your ability to react consciously is intensified and you are freer to make deliberate choice about how to respond to clients. Only by knowing yourself are you in a position to make active and creative use of feelings, thoughts, intentions, and motives to optimize the helping process. Francisco, for example, found it nearly impossible to non-punitively tolerate any adult client who abused a child. He would immediately associate this to his own background of being beaten and lose his professional objectivity, stability and ability to be consistently caring toward the client. Therapeutic errors frequently arise from such countertransference; however, they also can arise from lack of information about the client, from lack of adequate training, or even from poor timing or utilization of an intervention.

You need to open the way for yourself to examine your beliefs and attitudes, to find compatibility between them and feelings and behavior, to expose and to scrutinize your basic assumptions, and to search out who and what you really are. Such awareness leads to more disciplined and clearly directed work. Learn to avoid the pitfalls of omnipotence and countertransference. Touch your own feelings: those of being able or expected to solve all problems; those of being overwhelmed by elusive and unconscious responses to the client or those of being discouraged with reactions that seem uncooperative and ungrateful. All these feelings, when unexamined, lead to unwittingly reinforcing clients' feelings of passivity and helplessness. In honestly facing yourself, you are freed to attend to what is happening with the client.

In brief, do what you expect clients to do. Take a hard look at yourself. Through self-examination, discover, acknowledge, and accept yourself for who and what you are, alter what is possible and you will be better able to accept clients for who they are. Develop a realistic understanding of your world. Assume responsibility for your actions and reactions.

SEVEN LEVELS OF THE RELATIONSHIP

The effectiveness and success of the helping endeavor depends largely upon your ability to institute and to sustain a helping alliance with clients. This alliance is usually described in two ways: (1) as a means to sustain clients as they work on problems, or (2) as a prototype of the problems they may have in other relationships. The relationship is not just a way to manipulate clients to accept help. It is integral; therefore, when clients act towards you in ways that are inappropriate or self-defeating, you can comment on these behaviors. This provides the client with an opportunity to change his or her behavior with you and others in the world. These constructive changes in behavior can then become integrated into the client's regular patterns of behavior.

While there is general unanimity about the importance of human relationship in promoting growth and change, there is less common understanding about just *how* relationships promote such development. I characterize the "how" in terms of seven "I's" in dynamic interrelationship. They are in order (a) with the latter processes contingent upon the quality of the preceding ones and (b) of decreasing client awareness. The "I's" are: Individualization, Intellectual learning, Imitation, Internalization, Identification, Idealization, and Individuation. Each "I" is defined and described below and then illustrated with a case example based on the following vignette.

> Marta's two children, Jesus, 3, and Sonia, 2, were placed in foster care in a large metropolitan agency because of their father's repeated and brutal physical abuse. Marta was committed to doing all she could to have her children returned to her care now that Carlos, her partner, had died of AIDS.
>
> Marta, 19 years old, had lived in foster care most of her own childhood because of her mother's mental illness and father's desertion. She loved her children and was highly motivated to reach her goal.
>
> Marta, Jesus and Sonia all test HIV positive, although none have symptoms.

Individualization

Individualization is the process of individualizing the client, focusing upon this particular person rather than on his/her problem, or on this person as representing a whole class of people. It involves recognizing and affirming clients and building upon their unique qualities, but, ironically, at the same time conveying the message that they are not alone with their troubles, either in the sense that others have suffered and overcome similar adversity, or that you are available to join them.

Bear in mind that many of your clients are demoralized. They have been emotionally if not physically battered. They have been browbeaten, rejected, mocked, and humiliated—even by people who called themselves helpers. Often, in the name of "help," clients have been labeled crazy, weak, stupid, selfish, or evil. Why should they believe that you will treat them differently? Why should they believe that you will try to see them for who they truly are? Respect the diversity and variety of individuals; do not stereotype them.

Individualization means accepting and appreciating the uniqueness and dignity of clients as separate and autonomous beings. Marta was responsive to help because she felt that for the first time a professional did not "speak down" to her, "like other caseworkers, as being some sort of worthless jerk," or cower for fear of contracting AIDS, or stereotype her as an unfit mother.

Intellectual Learning

Intellectual learning entails encouraging clients to consolidate and apply in the conduct of their daily lives new knowledge and skills developed in the helping process. Every action between you and the client creates structures and patterns of learning and awareness. At this level, the relationship involves the cognitive processes of learning and teaching. Its object is knowledge and skill enhancement. Within the context of the relationship, clients' perceptions about themselves, others, and their environment come under challenge. This challenge is cognitive in the sense that their ideas are questioned and they are encouraged to consider new ideas. At this level you appeal to their cognitive and conscious processes. You involve them in a dialogue where they become aware of untapped knowledge, ideas and strengths. Information is given, concrete suggestions and advice are provided, and direct guidance is offered. You provide a realistic view of the client's ongoing interactions with others and with the environment. The purpose is to nourish a sense of mastery over the rational and tangible aspects of their situation. A further purpose is to alert them to habitual patterns of self-loathing and self-blame that cause still further self-defeating reactions to life.

In the role of teacher and coach, you provide technical assistance for developing and improving skills in problem solving and decision making and assisting clients to recognize the impact of their "self" on that process. You do this by asking key questions, providing new experiences, highlighting inconsistencies, suggesting modifications, reframing (i.e., helping clients to see their situation in a different way), focusing, and contracting. Ask clients to look at and talk about themselves and their dilemmas. Intellectual understanding is a necessary component. It bolsters decision-making and problem-solving skills but focuses on increased self-appraisal. Marta, for example, listened attentively to my direct instructions about legal steps and parental skills necessary to be met to ensure her children's return. She acted on each one of them closely following the suggestions offered. Each step she made, to assure medical screening, to find adequate housing, and to enroll in a parenting workshop, reinforced a sense of accomplishment.

Imitation

Imitation is a process in which clients deliberately emulate or simulate what they perceive as positive in your interactions with them. At this third level of relationship, you continually demonstrate your competence to clients. This involves clients' directly observing if you practice what you preach in your dealings with them. They observe you closely in your dealings with them, with other clients, staff and colleagues. Inevitably appraising your ability to facilitate communication, manage anxiety, encourage mutuality, and foster cooperation in working together, they ask themselves, "Do you demonstrate yourself to be the kind of person who will hear me?" "Will you help me feel trust, encourage me to open up?" "Are you keenly attuned to timing; are you sensitive and aware of nuances?" "Do you identify and verbalize tension openly and deal with it?" and "Do you display such characteristics as warmth, acceptance, respect, understanding, interest, tact, maturity, belief in your own ability to help, and trust?"

Your role at this level is that of a model. When clients sense your expertise, coupled with an intellectual understanding of the process, they are motivated toward imitation. They shape themselves to "take on" parts of you. Clients do not become clones; rather, they imitate your effective decision making, calmness, actions, and attitudes by adopting and adapting your compatible and favorable qualities into their own behavioral repertoire.

Imitation is reinforced when you share with clients how they themselves and what is happening affects you. Inquire about your impact on them. You model a way of operating which can effectively change clients' perspective and behavior. For example, quietly studying my nonpunitive interaction with Jesus and Sonia during interviews with the family, Marta adopted as her own my style of selecting alternative non-verbal activities for Jesus and Sonia, of non-physically disciplining the children, and of rewarding their "good" behavior. Awkward and stilted at first in the way she copied me, practice and the positive results she got made it easier to make it more naturally her own.

Internalization

Internalization, the fourth interconnected level, involves clients making the goals, attitudes and behaviors you reflect toward them in the relationship an integral part of themselves. It pertains, in other words, to your management of the relationship itself. This involves mutual reflection on your exchange with clients and how you handle the dynamics of this encounter.

Reduce anxiety and convey an atmosphere of trust. Invite clients to share their reflections and introspections about themselves, but, more importantly, about this immediate relationship. Encourage clients to experience, examine and ultimately talk about the problems, strains and tensions in your relationship with them. Open discussion creates an atmosphere of mutuality and collegiality. It promotes reflection about the meaning and the mechanics of establishing and maintaining functional relationships. Through this kind of dialogue you assist clients in liberating themselves from rigid or stereotyped responses that limit them. In a climate of acceptance and honesty, you open channels to explore together such questions as, "What can we gain from this experience together?" and "What can we give to each other?" Building a warm, supportive environment with a sense of security leads you to an alliance that eventually permits the expression of clients' doubts and apprehensions without fear of harsh judgment.

Clients' habitual ways of relating to others and their ingrained ways of looking at themselves in relation to others is re-enacted in their relationship with you. They can experience you in the same way in which they experience others in the present and have experienced others in the past. Most significantly, they can experience you in ways in which they have never experienced before. Likewise, they can experience themselves in relationship to you in ways with which they are familiar and, at the same time, in ways in which they have never felt before.

Understand clients' repetition of the past-in-the-present, but provide a special interpersonal experience and environment in which change can take place. Illumination occurs in the context of this new and uniquely experienced relationship. It results in clients losing the attraction of old ways and the concomitant development of a more adaptive stance.

No significant human relationship proceeds without conflict, stress, and stalemates. These are interspersed, as well, by periods of both rapid and barely discernible change and times of confidence and of doubt. Moderate these shifts to prevent them from constituting a threat or arousing intolerable uncertainty. By doing so, your clients learn to tolerate and reasonably well integrate them as integral to the overall harmonious functioning of this, as well as all, relationships.

In this relationship, anger can be expressed and responded to without overwhelming anxiety. It can be reasonably resolved collaboratively. Encourage mutuality and reciprocity so that barriers become foci for examination and growth rather than impenetrable walls.

Throughout life we all need to interchange our observations with others in order to sustain our level of functioning. Clients achieve the capacity to integrate new experiences with you into a meaningful system by practicing the sharing of perceptions with you. It helps them develop what has traditionally been referred to as an observing ego.

Your role is that of medium — a channel of deep expression and responsiveness. Immediacy and self-disclosure about your reactions to them enhances understanding of the therapeutic process. It fortifies clients' recognition of triggers of their own intensive emotional reactions in this as well as in other relationships. In a way, clients, without conscious plan or cognizance, take "in" a part of you. This firsthand experience of rapport leads clients to a more relevant inquiry and critical analysis of their own contribution to the helping procedure. The very process of gaining this relationship with you inducts them into perceiving and understanding better who they *are*. They discover and then develop control of their own responses.

Immersion in the evolution and consolidation of the relationship propels clients toward arriving at a heightened understanding of themselves and the forces that operate in their lives. They assimilate and integrate your manner which alters the way they interact with others. Encouraged to verbalize her introspections about herself as she participated in the helping relationship, Marta became aware that her way of interacting with me and with others had altered. She became less suspicious of others' motives and more willing to trust that their assisting her in various concrete ways — accompanying her to welfare centers, giving her clothing, and babysitting, arose from good intentions, not necessarily from ulterior motives. She recognized that the helping relationship had corrected her usual perception of herself and others in relationship.

Identification

Identification involves clients taking in as a permanent part of their personality structures the attributes, characteristics and values they detect in you as you interact with them. The fifth significant level of relationship, it is less conscious than are the four others already discussed. Identification involves the way you establish an alliance, stay optimally in touch with the clients' experiences and handle their vulnerability within it. It entails clients' exquisite sensitivity to your empathic resonance, your response to their subjective experience, and the way you convey understanding of their feelings, attitudes and ideas. Clients experience, absorb, or "soak up" the way in which you empathize with them and establish the core conditions for change.

For many clients, suitable objects for identification have been unavailable. For others there have been impairments or interruptions in their relationships making the necessary identifications impossible to achieve. You are in a position to correct this privation. Provide a positive outlook and a less self-critical attitude along with an opportunity for introspection and reflection.

You serve as a mentor for clients. What cannot be conveyed in direct ways, is incorporated by association. The way you manage your complex mixture of roles, tasks, and emotions instructs them, but, more importantly, it impels them toward greater compassion for and acceptance of their own. How you relate to clients exposes them to a broader array of adaptable and acceptable behaviors to practice for themselves.

Clients are exquisitely aware of your communications and your mistakes. The way in which you "tune in" to them, and to yourself, reflects back their emotional and intellectual state, tracks the process of change, and shapes the organization of clients' selves. At a conscious and unconscious level, clients recognize your mode of interrelating which becomes an internal part of their own identity and structure. Over time their identifications become increasingly discriminate and focus on features and qualities that are compatible with and enhance their own. Your attributes and qualities are integrated and become transformed into the nucleus of their own being. With Marta, for example, responding with gentle warmth and acceptance to her deeply rooted self-doubts, and with empathy to her anguish associated with having abandoned her children the way she herself had been, she came to forgive herself. In a protected environment, with my expressing sympathy for her pain and sense of desperation, validating her experience, while conveying a matter-of-fact attitude about current and previous self-destructive behaviors, she eventually risked treating herself with the kindness, non-judgment and respect she experienced from me.

Idealization and Mirroring

Idealization and mirroring are interconnected processes. Idealization comprises your welcoming clients' admiration of and identification with you for strength and security and for confirming their own positive sense of self. Mirroring involves recognizing, approving and admiring clients' ability to grow independent and create something of value. This dimension of relationship is thoroughly unconscious. It emerges from your willingness to immerse yourself in their experience and your accessibility to and utilization of your own vulnerability within the context of the relationship. In addition to experiencing trust, warmth and empathy, clients "feel into" your conscious and disciplined attention. They experience the way you use your vulnerability and sensitivity in guiding them. As you transform your own vulnerability into awareness and creativity, you provide a mirror for them. Clients need to feel understood and affirmed for who they are, to feel safe and comfortable, to feel some degree of sameness or likeness with you and others. Some of these needs for validation and affirmation are met to a limited degree through your exposing them to challenging experiences, which, when they face, produce a deep sense of accomplishment and mastery. The relationship fulfills more of these through the process of mirroring.

Kohut has pointed out that the healthy adult needs the mirroring of the self by others and needs targets for idealization (Kohut, 1971). Clients internalize the function provided by the new self-object, you. They see you draw freely on your inner life which reinforces and corroborates their personhood. As you share your perceptions and subjective reactions, you free clients to expose theirs. You allow them to merge temporarily with you. In so doing, they receive an infusion of certainty and confidence. Provide clients with a vehicle to develop an internal means for maintaining esteem and for tolerating mistakes and failures. When clients become more certain of themselves they require your support less and feel increasingly confident without your affirmation. Clients thus come to reach into themselves for the validation you initially provided.

In terms of idealization, clients intercept and respond to your emotional accessibility to your own self as well as your availability to them. They wonder, "Do you emerge as a genuine and caring person?" and "Are you sufficiently integrated and free of your own 'stuff' to be available to me?" They are sensitive to your being able to engage in a deep interpersonal relationship without losing integrity or autonomy, allowing them to become less rigid and protective. They take into their self-structure the qualities you evidence and utilize them for inner regulation. Marta became severely depressed at the loss of her children and suffered from intense panic attacks, doubting every decision she made. Building on Marta's intellectual and nurturing capacity, I helped Marta to view the surrender of her children as a temporary and creative way to become a better mother. This intervention provided her with a new positive identity as a "succeeding" rather than a "failing" mother. Viewing herself as smart and loving, rather than stupid and unfeeling, relieved her anxiety and depression. Invited to participate in a group of mothers where she was dubbed the "expert," the gratification from her role as model augmented that from her new identity as "good" mother. Marta had merged with my belief in and validation of her, making it her own.

Individuation

Individuation results in clients separating from you as a consequence of their gaining, through the relationship, mastery over their own lives and concomitant higher self-esteem, the freedom to confront life's challenges on their own. Draw upon your capacity for empathic introspection as you attend to data that clients present. It will not only enable you to connect various elements of clients' current problems to the pattern of their life experience, but will intensify your fathoming their essence. In doing this, generally applicable explanations may elude you, but you will grasp the core of what makes them individually and uniquely themselves.

With this kind of responsiveness in the relationship, clients discover a new awareness of anxiety and a greater ability for self-control. They learn how to acknowledge and accept themselves and to understand and alter maladaptive behavioral patterns. More significantly, and perhaps ironically, through the relationship they come to increase their basic level of differentiation. The stabilization of your unique way of relating to each other in this special alliance forms and reforms their sense of autonomy and separateness. When you flexibly interact with clients, without fully gratifying or fully frustrating them, when you encourage, recognize, and reinforce their facing and mastering difficult internal impulses and external stresses increasingly on their own, you nurture integration and individuation. When you honor their taking increasing charge of their lives and they accept their own role in their progress and your gradual withdrawal from involvement with them, they gain an increased security in their own identity and autonomy and the capacity to preserve the distinction and separation between themselves and others. Improvement, therefore, does not depend on maintaining the relationship, but on your encouraging their accepting separation from it.

Marta succeeded in getting adequate public housing, arranging medical attention for herself, Jesus and Sonia, enrolling in training to become a legal secretary, having her children returned to her care and ending her work at the agency. Her progress dramatizes the power of the relationship for revising the image of oneself—Marta came to reject the picture of herself as insensitive, depriving or malevolent toward her children; for freeing one from self-defeating means of survival—she no longer desperately clung to familiar but destructive behaviors. Through the reliability, consistency, constancy and emotional resonance supplied by the relationship, she overcame her false "toughness" arising from premature maturity, and let down the facade of being "street smart" to taking pride in herself as being a self-governing, expert survivor.

Developing an adequate and autonomous sense of self then requires your suspending judgment and supplying

1. a holding environment or "safehouse" that allows for maximum emotional comfort and trust for clients
2. empathic resonance and response
3. sensitivity to clients' suffering
4. a stable and steady structure for self-exploration and practicing new behaviors

5. a balance of serious attentiveness and spontaneity in mutually searching for self-definition and healthier functioning
6. opportunity for identification with you
7. adequate experiences of caring, approval and achievement
8. tolerating their hostility and outbursts
9. support for their increasing independence of thinking and action.

Figure 5 is something I read that touched me greatly because it described in powerful terms what happens when these basics are ignored or forgotten.

FIGURE 5

To Be a Mental Patient

Rae Unzicker

To be a mental patient is to be stigmatized, ostracized, socialized, patronized, psychiatrized.

To be a mental patient is to have everyone controlling your life but you. You're watched by your shrink, your social worker, your friends, your family. And then you're diagnosed as paranoid.

To be a mental patient is to live with the constant threat and possibility of being locked up at any time, for almost any reason.

To be a mental patient is to live on $82 a month in food stamps, while your shrink drives a Mercedes Benz.

To be a mental patient is to take drugs that dull your mind, deaden your senses, make you jittery and drooling, and then be given more drugs to lessen the "side effects."

To be a mental patient is to apply for jobs and lie about how you've spent the last few months or years, because you've been in the hospital, and then you don't get the job anyway, because you're a mental patient.

To be a mental patient is to watch TV and see shows about how violent and dangerous and dumb and incompetent and crazy you are.

To be a mental patient is not to matter, to never be taken seriously.

To be a mental patient is to be a resident of a ghetto, surrounded by other mental patients who are as scared and hungry and bored and broke as you are.

To be a mental patient is to wear a label that never goes away, a label that says little about what you are and even less about who you are.

To be a mental patient is never to say what you mean, but to sound like you mean what you say.

To be a mental patient is to tell your psychiatrist he's helping you, even if he's not.

To be a mental patient is to act glad when you're sad and calm when you're mad.

To be a mental patient is to participate in stupid groups that call themselves therapy—music isn't music, it's therapy; volleyball isn't a sport, it's therapy; sewing is therapy; dish washing is therapy.

To be a mental patient is not to die—even if you want to—and not cry, and not hurt, and not be scared, and not be angry, and not be vulnerable, and not laugh too loud . . . because if you do, you only prove that you are a mental patient . . . even if you are not.

And so you become a no-thing, in a no-world, and you are not.

The helping relationship is a unique construction created by the mutual interaction between you and clients. Clients progress when you treat them in ways which substantially parallel the ways you encourage them to employ with others—family, friends, colleagues. Self-development and personal individuation are inextricably intertwined processes. They come to fruition in the relationship through seven interdependent processes I identify as Individualization, Intellectual understanding, Imitation, Internalization, Identification, Idealization and Individuation.

RELATIONSHIP: KEYSTONE OF HELPING

The relationship is the keystone of the helping process. Help involves two important components: (1) *what* is given, and (2) *how* it is given. "What" is discussed in other chapters. "How" is the very experiencing of the relationship. It is the quintessential learning experience. The immediacy of your presence and attitudes, rather than your skills or techniques, is the heart of helping. The relationship enables clients to learn how to observe themselves, and their capacity to integrate experiences into a meaningful system. The building and maintenance of the relationship not only facilitates clients' capacity for change. It *is* the change.

QUESTIONS TO ASK YOURSELF

I view the following ten questions, proposed some years ago by Carl Rogers (1958), as the most pertinent and eloquent ones available to guide you in helping.

1. Can I *be* in some way which will be perceived by the other person as trustworthy, as dependable, or consistent in some deep sense?
2. Can I be expressive enough as a person that what I am will be communicated unambiguously?
3. Can I let myself experience positive attitudes toward this other person — attitudes of warmth, caring, liking, interest, respect?
4. Can I be strong enough as a person to be separate from the other?
5. Am I secure enough within myself to permit him his separateness?
6. Can I let myself enter fully into the world of his feelings and personal meanings and see these as he does?
7. Can I receive him as he is? Can I communicate this attitude?
8. Can I act with sufficient sensitivity in the relationship that my behavior will not be perceived as a threat?
9. Can I free him from the threat of external evaluation?
10. Can I meet this other individual as a person who is in the process of *becoming*, or will I be bound by his past and by my past?

REFERENCES

Grunebaum, Henry. "Harmful Psychotherapy Experience," *American Journal of Psychotherapy*, XL (2), 1986.

Kadushin, Alfred. *Supervision in Social Work*. NY: Columbia University Press, 1976.

Kohut, Heinz. *The Analysis of Self*. NY: International Universities Press, 1971.

McCall, Ella. "I Tell Homeless Kids, 'Love You, Baby,'" *The New York Times*, November 1, 1988.

Mahler, Margaret et al. *The Psychological Birth of the Human Infant*. NY: Basic Books, 1975.

Marziali, Elsa, and Alexander, Leslie. "The Power of the Therapeutic Relationship," *American Journal of Orthopsychiatry*, 61 (3), July, 1991.

Rogers, Carl. "The Characteristics of a Helping Relationship," *Personnel and Guidande Journal*, 37 (1), 1958.

Unzicker, Rae. "To Be a Mental Patient," *Pilgrimage*, 14 (4), 1988.

Chapter VI

Assessment:
Learning from a Jigsaw Puzzle

We never see only what we see; we always see something else with it and through it! Seeing creates, seeing unites and above all seeing goes beyond itself.

— Paul Tillich

Not everything that is faced can be changed; but nothing can be changed until it is faced.

—James Baldwin

Clients are complex and multifaceted. Seldom, if ever, will you be able to pin one label on them that either completely satisfies you or fully describes them: that is a tribute to both of you. Clients, like you, are composed of many varied parts. Some of these were cut long ago; some of these continue to be shaped day by day; some of these have jagged edges, and some are smooth and curved. All of us continually try to figure out who we are and how we can fit the pieces of our lives together.

Think about your clients in ways that include a consideration of the multiple features of their life experience. As you endeavor to understand their stories, recognize that clients' life experiences get re-enacted with you. Take account, then, of the mold from which they were cut and how well their facets interface as you undertake "putting it all together." In a way, figuring out clients is much like solving a jigsaw puzzle. Seeking coherence needs to be your nagging preoccupation. Through assessment you bring all the seemingly disparate pieces together into a coherent whole.

WHY IS ASSESSMENT IMPORTANT?

Accuracy and sensitivity in assessment, to a large measure, contributes to your therapeutic effectiveness. It guides inquiry into the fullness of clients' lives and helps you to select and continually monitor your interventions. It guides you in the immediate and delicate interactions with clients. It is integral to the entire helping process.

Assessment is ongoing. It is not merely a formal statement, an end-product after a prescribed period of time. It requires time taken together with clients that allows both of you to pause, reflect, and re-evaluate. Certainly, at the end of each encounter and at pre-set and spontaneous intervals along the way, you summarize progress and take stock once again of where you are going; but, in truth, you are assessing from moment to moment.

Why is assessment important? It enables you to avoid the mistake of assuming that only you are in charge of the change effort. Both you and client work hard and do independent thinking. In the end, the soundness of assessment depends upon how well your thinking meshes.

Assessment focuses on clients, their problems, the helping situation, and on you. Things do not move in a straight line from cause to effect. Problems result from complicated interactions among numerous variables. Clients are influenced by many things, and are neither determined nor cured by any one thing. To seek a single cause dooms you to failure.

Determining what is to be avoided and what is to be supported, what is to be strengthened and what is to be altered, are all vital functions of assessment. In clearly identifying sources of pain and anxiety, assessment prevents you from having things go from bad to worse by rushing in to fix them too quickly without full awareness of what you are dealing with. Often, in the rush to make things better, you may reinforce clients' old patterns and promote their carrying forward unresolved issues which then further overwhelm them. Assessment is also important because it locates attributes and capabilities to be tapped in enhancing clients' potential.

If all these reasons are not enough, assessment is important because it helps:

— ascertain the nature of the person;
— specify the nature of the problem;
— differentiate attitudes toward self, family, and environment;
— name motivational forces;
— describe the reality of their experience;
— identify what is normal, healthy, and positive;
— select what is possible and practical;
— locate barriers to change;
— detect resources available for overcoming barriers;
— characterize resistant factors;
— determine prognosis;
— determine the frequency of appointments;
— estimate the duration of the helping process;
— set the tempo of the work;
— decide the modality and method of intervention;
— predict the consequences of one change to others that might come later;
— evaluate the efficacy of the intervention.

Obviously, assessment is simultaneously a process of elimination, of ruling things *out*, as well as a process of assignation, or pulling things *in*.

Assessment provides an overall picture, not just a classification, that permits clients and you to evaluate the extent to which goals have been reached and the degree to which change is enduring. It is an opportunity for you to assemble and order pieces together and, ultimately, to make decisions about terminating your work together.

WHAT ASSESSMENT IS NOT

Consider, for a moment, what assessment is *not*. It is neither a reductionistic "pigeonholing" of pathology or problems nor a labeling from some typology or classification system, although that might be one step in it. Assessment is, rather, a humble attempt at comprehensive discernment of the overall nature of clients. It is an appreciative, holistic look at human beings in all their complexity, singularity, and dignity.

Assessment is not a one-sided abstract opinion delivered by you, the expert. Rather, it involves interactional collaboration in which clients participate actively in a feedback process that

F ocuses on what is changeable;
E xtends and shares parts of each of you;
E licits feelings, reactions, suggestions and questions;
D escribes rather than confines, judges or interprets;
B uilds on honesty and openness;
A llows time and space for thorough consideration;
C oncentrates on and reinforces observable changes and
K nits secure relationships.

Assessment is not a restrictive intellectual exercise arriving at an analytical inventory or list of problems, but is an inclusive discriminating depiction of a whole which is not fixed or static. It is a flexible and dynamic process that changes as clients grow and change.

Not simply a retrospective account of what happened long ago and far away, assessment incorporates a prospective view of what is hoped for. A view from the past juxtaposed against a view of the future rounds out the picture of clients' present life situation. When assessing clients, respect the continuity of their lives.

LEARNING FROM A JIGSAW PUZZLE

Doing an assessment is much like doing a jigsaw puzzle. The end result is finding unity in the face of apparent fragmentation. The challenge is to bring the pieces together into a coherent whole. Your task, in brief, is to "put it all together." Figure 6 is an illustration of a finished puzzle.

Imagine the pieces of a jigsaw puzzle as if it were dumped haphazardly, scattered on a table. An accurate analogue of clients' lives in crisis, to begin putting it together demands a creative mentality, enthusiasm, and patience. As with clients, clarity about your own role, values, and intentions as well as confidence that there is some solution, that it *can* be put together, encourages success. Assessment also requires the confidence that clients have the capacity to

FIGURE 6

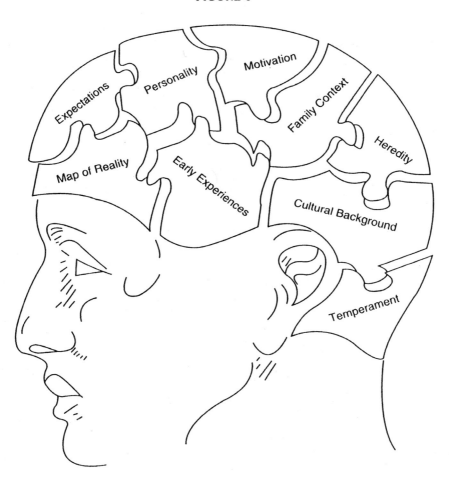

change and to grow. It also requires your engrossment in the process. At first, you might recognize isolated bits, but rarely an amalgamated whole. How can the puzzle best be solved?

Puzzles are usually solved using a combination of intellect (science) and intuition (art). A sprinkling of inspiration (spirit), enthusiasm, and creativity also help. Working from the left brain, you draw upon logic in reasoning how various pieces might fit together and you calculate next steps using a linear, sequential, and inductive approach. Simultaneously, working from the right brain, you draw upon intuition.

Select a starting point. Take a cursory overview to locate similar pieces and then collect and assemble them. These pieces are combined into piles of like size, shape, color and impression. The next step involves finding pieces with clear boundaries, usually straight edges which, joined together, give the outer border. It is extraordinarily difficult, if not impossible, to "put it all together" without first discovering the outer framework. These edges make it possible to direct attention inward. Such a frame makes the puzzle less elusive, clarifies the broad outline of the basic pattern, and allows you to visualize how the whole might finally appear. You cannot solve the puzzle without first accepting limitations imposed by the framework.

With clients too, assessment involves sizing up their external reality, situational, social, and cultural factors. Develop a structure and an organized strategy for determining what to look for next.

As you proceed with the sometimes boring and time consuming task of actually piling similar pieces together, you begin to discover a basic pattern, the relationship of parts to each other, and to the whole. You begin to recognize how the parts intertwine and interrelate and sometimes converge. It is seldom as simple as it seems.

Take your time. Hurrying, scrambling to put pieces together only increases frustration. Examine what you have before you. Clarify and reformulate the information. Make a continuous endeavor to look for the internal continuum, the interface, the link between discrete pieces.

Take close account of negative space. In other words, infer what probably is missing by studying the gaps in the puzzle. Look for them. Take stock of what pieces are missing, so you have a clue about what might fit. As with a jigsaw puzzle that you work on without benefit of the finished likeness, you may at first know only where to explore, not what you will find. Even when a piece is missing from the image, it is still possible to have a rather accurate, though incomplete, representation of the whole. Very often, patience with this sequence gives you a clearer hypothesis or sense of the whole. Step away from it for a while; put the puzzle aside.

When you return to the puzzle, get more information, gather more pieces, rearrange them based on fresh impressions. Be open to serendipitous discoveries. You may discover, by accident, that some fit. Do not force pieces together that do not interlock easily or smoothly; they were not meant to fit. You will fail to capture the puzzle's unique design. Although some areas of the puzzle will come together almost spontaneously, for the most part, success in completing it depends upon your tolerating uncertainty and persistent hard work.

You will not triumph over the chaos until you discover the basic relationships among pieces. Progress may at first be uneven. Indeed, along the way, you may face what seem to be insuperable barriers posed by clients, circumstances, or you. Pieces may be misplaced. The table may be jarred. You may lose interest or be distracted. Stay with it. As you relate parts to whole, a more congruent picture emerges, giving you increased confidence that it is coming together.

Gradually you will discern the context and character of the larger picture. This informs your next move and makes it easier to fill in the inner core. The final solution unifies what at first seemed to be disjointed details.

There is a point at which the puzzle metaphor breaks down. With clients, as sometimes with a puzzle, you do not have an image of the final picture in front of you. The puzzle is fixed and static, with but one solution: clients, on the other hand, are in constant flux and there is always the potential for new elements. The continuous circular movement of exchange between clients and you influences not only each of you reciprocally, but the end result as well. Clients are not completely determined by their context and actively contribute to determining their characteristics and movement.

Where the puzzle analogy breaks down further is that total success with a jigsaw puzzle requires restoring it to its original form. Success with clients, on the other hand, often means the construction of a new reality, a redefinition of self, or an expansion of boundaries. With clients you act as a catalyst in the search for new connections, deeper meanings and unexpected answers.

As with any puzzle, time, experience, practice and experimentation help make it possible to absorb and code information faster, bringing solutions more quickly into awareness.

Here, in summary, are tips for approaching client assessments or puzzles:

1. You cannot know how much you do not know so begin with a sense of not knowing, being open to discovery.
2. Get as many perspectives on the puzzle as possible; recognize all the various combinations because you cannot imagine what you may find.
3. For each combination, formulate alternate views; feel bold about looking, providing you do not already think you have figured it out.
4. Consider the function of each of the pieces in relation to those around it.
5. Think of assessment as involving phases or intermittent bursts of work, so that factors that elude you at first later can be successfully discovered and explored.

THE GENERAL PROCESS OF ASSESSMENT

Assessment is a tandem process with constant interplay and interdependence between clients and you, much like that of a wheel where the movement of the hub, rim and spokes are interdependent. This is illustrated in Figure 7.

TYPES OF ASSESSMENT

There are many types of assessment — popular and informal, professional and formal, reliable and unreliable.

Popular and Informal Instruments and Techniques

Some of the more popular types of assessment appear regularly in self-help books, magazines, and newspapers; sometimes they even appear in professional journals. They take the form of self-reporting questionnaires, indexes, profiles, and forms. Various procedures

FIGURE 7. The Tandem Process of Assessment

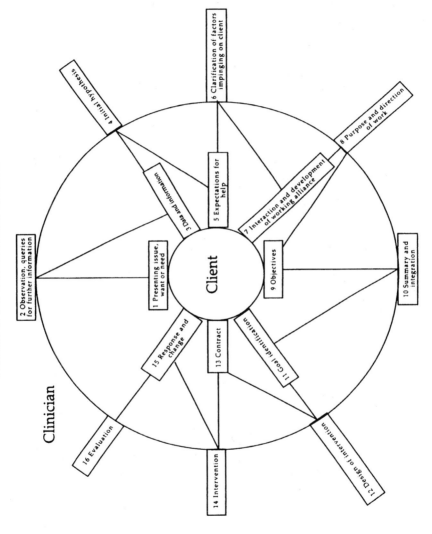

attempt to assess personality based on unusual and unexpected factors. For example, the Luscher Color Test attempts to analyze personality using information on color likes and dislikes. It has even been argued that "You Are What You Laugh At." *The New York Times* (Tuesday, August 30, 1983) reported the development of a sense of humor test "intended to shed light on the fundamental nature of human personality."

While some of these may have some measure of validity and may indeed provide an accurate portrait of one aspect of clients, beware! For the most part they are mechanistic and simplistic and can in and of themselves reveal little. Their danger is that little may be taken as a lot. They can, however, be fun, even revealing. Engaging your client in them can be enjoyable for the two of you. What they say about assessment and the very way clients respond to them provide invaluable clues for augmenting your face-to-face assessment.

Games too, like the "Ungame," can offer incisive information about clients. Do not hesitate to use these, discriminatingly, recognizing their limitations. You are more likely to use them successfully, however, when you know their shortcomings and fallacies, and when you leave yourself open to the unexpected. Games can be rich sources of information as they break routine. When you deliberately and knowingly suspend rules, clients sometimes reformulate established ways of behaving and rediscover truths already known or discover new ones. Variety, seeing clients from as many angles and under as many circumstances as possible, can help you get a more complete and well-rounded image of them. Avoiding conventional and stereotyped methods generates more distinct portraits of clients. Creative viewpoints and solutions often come from unexpected juxtapositions, strange combinations, and odd connections. Playing the game "Monopoly," for example, helped to put Jose into sharper focus and helped him to see his own behavior as others saw it.

> Jose was an exceptionally bright 12-year-old who was not liked at all by his peers. It had reached the point that they were making their dislike very clear to him by continually teasing and taunting him. At a time when peer acceptance was para-

mount, he seemed only to do things that intensified his rejection.

As part of our work, we began an ongoing game of Monopoly. Diagnostically it provided a look at Jose's behavior both when things were going his way and when they were not. It allowed us to examine his behavior in response to his feelings. By mirroring his and modeling my behavior, he was able to see what others might feel in response to his gloating, crowing, bullying, whining, cheating and insulting behavior. It allowed him to come to terms with his competitiveness. It provided impetus to talk philosophically about winning in the short run and losing in the long.

Professional and Formal Instruments and Techniques

You are probably familiar with some of the more common forms of psychological testing for personality and intelligence. Just peruse a psychological assessment catalogue. The tests, profiles and scales mirror every theory—Freudian, Jungian, Adlerian; reflect every modality—individual, group, family; trace every approach—cognitive, affective, behavioral. Examine them closely. Each captures one element of truth.

Tests are available to measure intelligence, attitude, achievement, developmental patterns, aptitude, adaptive behavior, and even suicidal ideation. Some are pencil and paper, others scantron. Some are objective, others projective. Some are taken in isolation; others in groups. Some require an observer, others are self-administered. Some are self-scored, others are scored by computer. Some use no words, but utilize drawings or blocks instead; others are verbal. Assessment and diagnostic tests come in a wonderful and endless variety. Some are named for their developers, for places where they were developed, or for the rating technique used to score them. Others are acronyms.

The following litany is but a small sample of assessment instruments that are widely available: The Rorschach, TAT, MMPI, Wexler, Myers/Briggs Indicator, Q-Sort Technique, Stanford-Binet, Wechsler-Bellevue, WAIS-R, Cognitive Abilities Test, California Achievement Tests, Iowa Tests of Basic Skills, and Person/

Tree/House. These can be of considerable value in refining your understanding of clients. The limitation of such instruments, however, is that they are usually extrinsic to your actual work. In other words, they are "applied to" clients, independent of your exchange.

Do not mistake a unidimensional profile for a full picture. All these instruments are of assistance in more completely understanding clients. They amplify understanding, but they are not substitutes for your immediate clinical observations.

These instruments can be intrusive, and for this reason, use them selectively. Employ them when you need to answer questions or fill in important gaps that cannot be obtained in more direct and interactive ways. You may notice over time that these tests very often will confirm some of your own impressions. Take that as a sign of your clinical acuity.

Secondhand reports are another source of qualitative data. Reports from other professionals from the same or other disciplines can be of great value. Take them as suggestive and instructive, rather than definitive. Consider them for what they are: auxiliary sources of information. Consider them in a serious light, but do not allow them to prejudice your judgment or predispose you toward a particular stance that overshadows your own.

Use what is of benefit from all forms of assessment, but not at the expense of participating with clients as they unfold their life stories. When you include all relevant data, direct and inferential, in perspective, you will generate a more complete and accurate assessment. Employ a range of data sources — those already mentioned combined with autobiography (described and illustrated in Chapters VII & X), drawings (described with case examples in Chapter IX), logs (described with case illustrations in Chapter X), family trees (described at length in Chapters VIII & IX), and inventories (described with examples in Chapter IX).

No one method of assessment can measure or interpret the whole person. Each, taken alone, can diminish clients by reductionistically mistaking a narrow view for the wider panorama. Taken together, they provide a balanced, integrated, and comprehensive picture of the whole person. This comprehensive look at clients helps to ensure that you do not see the problem presented merely as a reflection of a client's personality deficiency.

Person-to-person collaboration gives you a formidable portrait of the underlying themes and repeating issues in clients' lives. In many ways, your best tactic is to learn the tools of a good investigative reporter who asks, "Who, What, Why, When and Where?" There is a definite advantage to this "hands-on" approach. It adds freshness and immediacy to the work. Assessment is integral and incorporated into rather than separate from the ongoing transactions between you. Furthermore, it can be fun. You will learn and appreciate what makes clients laugh as well as cry. Seeing them from as many vantage points as possible will make them more real and make the work lively for both of you. It will motivate and possibly strengthen clients' self-healing potential. That's quite an accomplishment.

WHAT'S IN A LABEL?

There is considerable controversy among helping professionals about the appropriateness of diagnostic labeling. Although there seems to be general agreement that effective treatment depends upon accurate evaluation of clients and their life situations, concerns are expressed about the degree to which categorizing and labeling clients—as schizophrenic, borderline, developmentally disabled, delinquent or unemployable actually creates stigma and limits opportunities. Other criticisms of assessment and diagnostic labeling approaches include their unintentionally or intentionally distorting facts or dynamics; overemphasizing pathology and overlooking attributes; ignoring multidimensional contextual information and lacking theoretical integration. All these challenge the viability of ensuring comprehensive treatment and planning based on accurate assessment and diagnosis. There clearly is no consensus about the critical focus and means of labeling.

Although a label can be limiting, respect its value for what it does tell you. Appreciate, as well, that a label pinned on a client shapes or alters your relationship.

A label helps you to name things, gives you some sense of control. There are, however some dangers in labeling. A label poses a risk of reification—that is, treating an abstraction as if it actually exists. A label may also give you a false sense of comfort or security, that simply by knowing the label you understand all that you are dealing with. Once a label is affixed, it is extremely difficult to remove it and it can stigmatize when it no longer applies. The danger, too, is that a label may stereotype and thereby shape, rather than reflect, the client's personality or situation. In other words, it can create a self-fulfilling prophecy.

When you purchase a sweater, for example, the label will give you quite a bit of information: its size; place of origin; whether the fabric is hand-or-machine woven; whether the material is new or processed. It fails, however, to tell you about texture, pattern and quality. Like a sweater label, a client label tells you facts but fails to capture essence, resilience, integrity, and again, quality. These can be determined and appreciated only by careful observation and handling. Such features are not identified on the label, nor can they be, for they are subtle yet substantive elements that defy easy depiction. Yet they are precisely the factors that, to a large measure, determine whether the sweater will wear well.

Some people never look at a label. They believe that it reveals nothing of true value and is intended just to placate an easily fooled consumer. But the label gives instructions about care that cannot be discovered in any other way. Do not hesitate to look at a label. Get a "feel" for the material. Try it on to see if it fits. Turn it inside out to scrutinize its construction.

What has a sweater label to do with client assessment? The comparison is quite appropriate, with an important exception. Sweater labels, even though deficient, better characterize garments than client labels characterize people. People labels tend to emphasize what is wrong rather than what is right. They are distillations of clinicians' conceptions, reworkings of clients' accounts rendered in jargon. The jargon, however, constrains and trivializes clients. When we stray so far from sources and reduce complex phenomena to shorthand, communication certainly becomes more efficient; but the essence of clients is compromised, perhaps lost. People labels are superficial and cannot give instructions for care. They reveal what is on the surface—and often mask clients' subjective experience of their distress and the way they cope with it. If you take labels to be more than they are, your perception will be distorted and limited; the way you interact with clients will be slanted and incomplete.

Do not settle for a label. Do not ignore or discard it either. A label tells something relevant. It tells one part of a larger story. It helps you to make sense out of the information you have; be mindful, however, that in using it, you are always dealing with a version of reality and not absolute truth. When combined with other labels and viewpoints, especially your own, it can have a further benefit. Your clients deserve your most thorough, inclusive, and far-reaching assessment. As with any procedure, labeling can be used positively or negatively — it is the care you take in its use that determines whether the outcome is helpful or hurtful to clients.

The next two chapters, VII and VIII, interface with each other, using the same case study to illustrate the benefit of integrating individual and family approaches in assessment and intervention. Chapter VII concentrates on individual diagnosis, examining the place of *The Diagnostic and Statistical Manual of The American Psychiatric Association III-R*, and reviewing the theoretical underpinnings and dimensions of individual assessment. Chapter VIII presents various facets of family assessment and proposes the genogram as a useful tool for both individual and family assessment.

Chapter VII

Models of Helping:
Working with an Individual

remember one thing only: that it's you — nobody else — who determines your destiny and decides your fate. nobody else can be alive for you nor can you be alive for anyone else.

—e.e. cummings

. . . the purpose of life, after all, is to live it, to taste and experience it to the utmost, to reach out eagerly and without fear for newer and richer experience . . . . The experience can have meaning only if you understand it. You can understand it only if you have arrived at some knowledge of yourself . . . .

— Eleanor Roosevelt

This chapter, the first of two devoted to individual and family assessment respectively, concentrates on models of personal and interpersonal elements of individual assessment and intervention. It then describes interventions based upon such assessment.

The helping process is greatly improved when assessment is precise and multi-dimensional. Clients' distress is caused by many things. Take note of as much of what constitutes their inner and outer lives as possible. Problems result from interacting intrapsychic and interpersonal processes that stimulate and reinforce each other. It is easy to forget that the functioning of a family as a whole is the product of individual processes and that, reciprocally, the functioning of individuals is influenced by their families. There is a tendency to emphasize one frame of reference or the other, individual or family, when doing an assessment or implementing a change effort. The truth is that they are compatible and complementary units of attention. When you are doing an assessment, ignore neither individuals' subjective experience nor their family system. Change in one foments change in the other. If you incorporate both into your work, synergy results.

In order to enliven the presentation, the story of Elaine precedes an overview of how three different major contemporary theories— Psychodynamic, Existential and Behavioral—conceptualize individual assessment and intervention. Brief sketches of each of these theoretical orientations are followed by a vignette describing how each might approach work with Elaine. A mnemonic abridgment distilling the principal concepts of each theory into a list of five "C's" concludes each section. These theoretical summaries are in no way exhaustive or inclusive. Their intent is to highlight how these three theories conceptualize assessment and intervention. After discussing the three models, I offer my own, including a list of ten "S's," which comprise factors that I consider when assessing and working with individuals. Integrating the three theories highlighted above, together with Ego- and Self-psychology concepts, into one inclusive guideline, provides a way to incorporate the dynamic interaction among the myriad of biological, cognitive, emotional, and cultural ingredients which influence individuals.

ELAINE'S STORY

Elaine, a thirty-year-old certified special education teacher from an upper-middle class background, was referred by a friend because of her serious dejection and talk of suicide. She herself reported feeling depressed and anxious. Elaine had moved to New York City three months previously from a midwestern rural area where she had lived for two years in a religious commune while finishing her graduate study in education.

Three months before first seeing me, Elaine had left her home following the death of her lover with whom she had had a clandestine affair.

Although Elaine was not presently suicidal, she was despondent and viewed herself as inept, of little worth, and "bad." She saw herself and her situation as unalterable. The only relief she found from her pervasive sense of sadness was reading and engaging in selected handicrafts such as tatting and macramé. She was able, too, to find support, and a little solace, from one or two trusted friends. She was skeptical that any intervention could be helpful. Evaluation of risk factors, resources and life-style did not indicate a need for immediate protective care, although the possibility, initially, was considered.

While Elaine suffered a series of recent losses, there was no premeditation or specific plan for suicide. Likewise, she reported no new symptoms, had a few friends available, and demonstrated little tendency toward impulsive behavior. She indicated that she wanted to give herself at least a "fair chance," and agreed to psychiatric evaluation.

Developmental history revealed that Elaine had been in therapy four times and hospitalized twice during adolescence for serious depression and suicide threats. She suffered recurrent episodes of distress and discouragement. Recalling that all during her teens, through to the present, she felt intense self-hatred and unworthiness, she now often saw herself as despicable and continually apologized for herself.

Elaine would follow the mention of every difficulty with an expression of regret either for "having" it or for talking about it. She was "sorry" that she would bolt up at five in the morning and was not able to get back to sleep. She felt terrible for "whining" about her loss of energy, lack of attention, melancholy. She continually reproached herself for referring to these difficulties as if they were "problems" and felt "awful" and guilty for exposing to me defects in her discipline or "faith" not being able to resolve such "frivolous" problems on her own.

Her memory of the past was scant. Chapter VIII describes how it was expanded using a family systems orientation. Elaine did acknowledge her strict religious upbringing as having contributed to her difficulty. She was raised in a modern faith fellowship which emphasized humility, being "perfect," doing what the Bible says, and leading a life of self-sacrifice, service, and simplicity. Even though she was educated to be an enabler within the religious sect, seeking help for herself represented all that she was raised to abhor and reject. It was to her, at minimum, self-indulgent and self-centered. It violated all beliefs she held dear; it bordered on the "sinful."

Always educated in religious schools, Elaine had spent all of her high school, college and graduate school years living in a faith community with her religiously fervent grandparents, who were more conservative than were her parents. Conformity was obligatory.

Suffering the loss of her lover and severing all ties to her family and religion, Elaine sheared her hair, never before cut, and came to "Sin City," ostensibly for a good teaching job. Now "freed," she felt herself, ironically, "imprisoned."

Despite her despairing presentation of self, Elaine manifested strength and resilience in more than a few areas of her life. Her keen intelligence and sensitivity were drawn upon and expanded during the course of the helping endeavor. For example, she learned early in her life to fulfill her unmet social and emotional needs by contact with teachers and older children. Solitary fantasy play as well as precise handiwork gave her a sense of accomplishment and mastery. Her thoughts, impressions and emotions were recorded in lengthy childhood diaries, which she still possessed, and made available to me. These entries are described at length in Chapter X, devoted to writing as an integral part of the helping process. Concentrating and embellishing on some of these earlier gains provided renewed energy to break the inertia she felt about getting "hold" of herself.

Elaine's likely genetic susceptibity to depression, combined with early traumatic experience, such as the emotional unavailability of her mother (later confirmed while doing family-oriented treatment), and an inability to influence or control significant events in her life, undermined her sense of self. Her present losses — home, lover, and grandparents, placed cruel demands on her already vulnerable ego.

THE PSYCHODYNAMIC MODEL
OF INDIVIDUAL ASSESSMENT AND INTERVENTION

Implicit in the psychodynamic approach (Alexander, Brenner, Fenichel, Hall, A. Freud, S. Freud, Hartmann, Shapiro), is a sense of determinism. Mental events are not viewed as random occurrences; rather, thoughts, feelings and impulses are considered to be causally related phenomena. Holding that crucial events of childhood generate conflicts which manifest and repeat themselves, unconsciously, in ongoing and present relationships, resolution of these intrapsychic conflicts comes only through a process of critical self-examination within a corrective emotional context. As insight is gained, light is shed on hidden conflicts thus enabling clients to deal with stresses in their lives less defensively and more rationally.

The process of assessment and intervention begins by establishing a relationship. In the psychodynamic perspective, your role in developing and maintaining the relationship provides both the context and means through which change occurs. In other words, clients' enhanced understanding of the relationship with you is applied to understanding aspects of their trouble in relationships with others. Psychodynamic clinicians say little about themselves, so whatever the client feels is the product of feelings associated with other significant people in the past which are projected onto them. They carefully monitor interactions with the client and seek to locate the sources of any confusion or anxieties in underlying fixed behavior patterns and early drives and wishes. The effectiveness of this approach relies a great deal on the phenomenon called "transference" — automatic attribution of attitudes, thoughts and feelings toward someone in the present which originated in early relationships with significant others, i.e., mother and father. As clients become more comfortable with you in the relationship over a long period of time, they begin to see you in a certain light, projecting onto you attributes that actually belong to a person in their past. These attributes trigger inappropriate reactions from clients and by subtle questioning and interpreting, you lead them to an emotional reeducation in which they learn more realistic perceptions and ways of behaving.

Because irrational forces are strong and conflicts remain largely out of awareness, it is through a deliberative process of "uncovering" that clients come to understand their sexual and aggressive impulses, environmental counterforces, and the particular interactions among the various agencies of the mind. In making an assessment, the psychodynamic clinician sketches a broad outline of the nature of clients' conflicts and studies clients' characteristic resistances (internal impediments interfering with or interrupting progress), transferences and defenses. Defenses are means, out of clients' realm of awareness, for controlling their anxiety by denying or distorting reality. Intervention is directed at enabling clients to reflect on possible original sources of underlying unconscious conflicts. The psychodynamic clinician, within the framework of the relationship, points out and explains the meaning and motivation behind these conflicts and interprets psychosexual developmental history and seeks to correct clients' distortions, reconstruct and analyze their repetitive patterns of reaction, recognize their dysfunctional defensive maneuvers against anxiety, and understand their early developmental experiences and personality structure. Clients' insight, combined with the clinician's analysis and interpretation, consolidates change.

A Psychodynamic Perspective on Elaine

Assessing Elaine from a psychodynamic standpoint requires careful consideration of her presenting problems. It also involves attention to her countenance and demeanor within the helping situation itself because this serves as a sample of her typical behavior. From her sketchy history, it seemed evident that attitudes toward herself were repetitions of internalized images from her past. Her depression was likely the result of having internalized depreciating views of her by her family, resulting in self-directed rage. Elaine's depression, in other words, could be viewed, in part, as a function of her aggressive instincts redirected against herself, possibly as punishment for harboring unacceptable wishes. Because her conflicts were buried deep in her unconscious, she could not recall precisely any outstanding events or "lessons" where they were evident.

Implicit, however, in her presentation of self was a sense of being inconsistently nurtured and of suffering emotional neglect and abuse. Her perception of herself as "bad," inadequate, and ugly, and her self-defeating behavior, which included self-denial, self-desertion, and turning against herself, reflected two significant dynamics. It mirrored treatment she likely received as a child. It also manifested her tendency to direct against herself the aggressive impulses she felt toward unavailable nurturing figures. A self-fulfilling prophesy resulted: out of fear, she did not "strike out," but felt guilty and punished herself repeatedly for negative feelings toward her parents and later for abandoning her religious foundations. She closed-off what she needed most—connection to others.

The traditional psychodynamic strategy for dealing with such depression relies on understanding defenses, transferences, and resistance through intrapsychic analysis and interpretation. To get at the root of the depression, its historical development must be fathomed, insight promoted; followed by giving expression to the rage. Rage, once expressed, externalized, and redirected to its appropriate source, brings relief.

The Psychodynamic "C's"

The following list encapsulates the critical elements of the psychodynamic approach to assessment and intervention. It is not intended to dilute the complexity, but, rather, to distill its essential features.

- Constitutional factors—heredity, biology and congenital factors
- Characteristic defenses including projection, denial, identification, rationalization, and sublimation
- Conflict sources in psychosexual development resulting in lack of resolution of normal crisis arising at each stage—oral, anal, phallic and genital
- Conscious/pre-conscious/unconscious factors
- Causation of basic personality patterns from family relationships in infancy and early childhood.

THE EXISTENTIAL MODEL
OF INDIVIDUAL ASSESSMENT AND INTERVENTION

Existentialists (Bugental, Frankl, Fromm, May, Yalom) deal with ultimate concerns — isolation, meaning, death, and freedom. The struggle with these concerns is seen as being at the core of clients' anxiety. Existentialists renounce the psychodynamic conceptualization of humans as driven by regressive forces and as subservient to unconscious aspects of themselves. Personal growth, will, choice in the face of despair, responsibility for the freedom of deciding one's fate, and the search for meaning, rather than intrapsychic conflicts or behavior, are central concerns to the existential clinician.

The existential view holds that the myriad of factors in an individual's life is too manifold to identify, much less to pinpoint, as causal. Past developmental history is not of primary concern: the here and now is. Indeed, the absence of prior information, the existentialist argues, allows more freedom to confront clients' present dilemmas. These dilemmas are assessed as arising from a sense of despair, loss of possibility, fragmentation and alienation of self, or lack of congruence with one's experience. While the psychodynamic clinician proposes that we are afraid of knowing our regressive tendencies, the existentialist proposes that we are afraid of knowing our progressive tendencies. Since humans are not static and are in a constant state of transition, and since they are inherently striving and self-affirming, no situation, however miserable, is a lost battle.

Postulating the *will* with its power to act, to feel and to organize experience, the existentialist directs efforts toward helping clients to open horizons and to release innate capacities by participating in the world of events. Intervention takes the form of an encounter in a dialectical process which brings clients to fuller awareness of themselves and their potential and their will in the face of uncertainty. The key factor is the relationship — an experience in form — in which clients can experience a new and constructive way of seeing and being with themselves and others.

Self-conscious decision making and self-direction make it possible for clients to transcend the immediate situation, to design their own lives, and to find meaning. The authenticity and spontaneity of the helping relationship itself, combined with dramatization and deep-experiencing of the here-and-now, actualizes clients' self-growth, self-determination, and self-responsibility. Existential clinicians use a variety of methods to identify and investigate maladaptive mechanisms. Techniques are borrowed from other approaches to relieve symptoms, but, more importantly, to enable clients to attain personal growth and mutually open relationships.

A unique feature of the existentialist perspective is the belief that both the clients and the helper can be changed by the helping relationship.

An Existential Perspective on Elaine

The existential viewpoint would not see Elaine's despair and anxiety as originating from suppressed instinctual drives or conflicts. Rather, her angst would be viewed as alienation between herself and the "givens" of her existence. Assessment would involve an in-depth understanding of Elaine's subjective experience which would free her capacity to rediscover meaning in her life and to stop numbing herself to her experience. Existentialists pay very little attention to external behavior. It is necessary to keep in mind that the feelings you perceive from her, as she describes her life, may not even remotely resemble her feelings as she perceives them.

This approach does not, as does the dynamic approach, aim at discovering signs of inferred states of intrapsychic conflicts or underlying disparities in affect, cognition and behavior. There are no prescribed procedures or techniques. Rather, the cardinal intervention entails helping Elaine contact her own inner experience. Flexible and versatile in approach, a variety of methods are employed, resting mainly on the strength and authenticity of the dynamic encounter with you. Within this relationship, Elaine is encouraged to contact the "present" from her own internal frame of reference, making her aware of her potential and possibilities, recognize authorship of her own life story, and take responsibility for editing and revising it.

The Existential "C's"

The list below captures the essential elements of the existential approach to assessment and intervention. It is intended to highlight its essential features, not to oversimplify them.

Consciousness — awareness of self, events, surroundings
Connection and commitment — to self and others
Continuum — the past, present, and future
Capacity to transcend immediate situation
Choice — liberating psychic immobility

THE BEHAVIORAL MODEL
OF INDIVIDUAL ASSESSMENT AND INTERVENTION

Behavioral theory (Bandura, Lazarus, O'Leary, Wolpe) rests upon the basic assumption that behavior is a function of its consequences and of modeling. We are both the product and producer of our environment. Since processes of the mind, e.g., defenses, transference, are neither observable nor amenable to scientific analysis, they are disregarded. Abnormal behavior is not viewed as necessarily pathological and is assumed to be acquired and maintained in the same way as normal behavior.

Behavioral assessment involves identifying the bond between anxiety and the stimuli evoking it.

In contrast to the psychodynamic and the existential orientation, the relationship is a deliberately structured learning alliance which develops in tandem with achieving identified goals. In other words, it is secondary, not essential, for desired change, and evolves from the integration of the contextual and interventive aspects of interactions.

Maladaptive learning is at the core of clients' problems. Behaviorists aver that clients learn a certain response and can unlearn it. Covert, unobservable needs, drives, motives, and wishes do not play a critical part although cognitive behaviorists suggest that a complex set of expectations, goals and values can be treated as behavior and have influence on performance. Maladaptive learning arises from involuntarily acquired, repeated, and reinforced response to stimuli in the environment. Successful change requires building an accurate and positive expectancy about results and structuring, rewarding, inhibiting or reshaping specific responses to anxiety producing stimuli. The behaviorist is active and directive and functions as a teacher or trainer using guided imagery, role-playing, self-monitoring and other techniques to learn more effective behavior. Clients repeat and practice these new alternative behaviors within and then outside the helping situation. Believing that insight is unnecessary, other techniques employed by behaviorists are desensitization (reconditioning to associate pleasant rather than anxious feelings to certain feared objects or events), shaping (altering behavior by reinforcing progressively closer approximations of the desired behavior), positive reinforcement (offering praise and social support), rehearsal of new behaviors, and coaching. A careful process of assessment precedes treatment and follows a contractual protocol which involves identifying and specifying the troublesome symptomatic behavior; identifying its antecedents, consequences, and frequency; specifying objectives; formulating a modification plan; substituting alternatives; repeating and practicing newly learned responses; rewarding achievements and evaluating change.

A Behavioral Perspective on Elaine

Elaine's depressive responses, according to a behaviorist, would be seen as a part of a complex, but circumscribed, stimulus-response chain. Indeed, the depressive responses themselves would be capable of stimulating the response chain. Behavioral assessment of Elaine would assume that her depressive behavior and symptoms were originally learned through operant conditioning and are presently maintained through the reinforcement of other people. To unlink the chain, identification and modification are required of the situations that reinforce responses. The behaviorist would also attempt to discriminate stimuli, i.e., events or behavior which precede feelings of depression or depressive behavior and utilize such techniques as desensitization, rehearsal, shaping and coaching combined with prescribed tasks. Positive reinforcement for successful task completion comes from the environment and from you, who become an activator and validator of new or changed responses.

The Behavioral "C's"

The list below identifies the major features of the behavioral approach to assessment and intervention.

— Components and specimens of behavior
— Controlling conditions of behavior
— Contingencies and constraints to change efforts
— Contracting for change
— Central learning mechanisms.

THE DSM III-R AND INDIVIDUAL ASSESSMENT

The DSM III-R is a comprehensive but controversial compendium for diagnosing individual problems in functioning. It is considered by many to be valid and reliable. Increasingly, it has become a standard tool for clinicians, educators, and researchers to arrive at commonly accepted descriptions and definitions of individual functioning.

Five years in development, the DSM III-R purports to take an atheoretical approach, incorporating several innovative features representing major advances in the field of mental health assessment. The authors believed that the inclusion of etiological theories would be an obstacle to the use of the manual by clinicians of varying theoretical orientations, since it would not be possible to present all reasonable etiological theories for each disorder described. Phobic Disorders, for example, are believed by some to represent a displacement of anxiety resulting from the breakdown of defensive operations for regulating internal unconscious conflict. Others explain phobias on the basis of learned avoidance responses to conditioned anxiety. Still others believe that certain phobias result from a disregulation of basic biological systems mediating separation-anxiety. In most cases, however, clinicians do agree on the clinical manifestations of phobia without agreement about its etiology.

Classification, therefore, is made on the basis of symptoms demonstrated by clients rather than on differing theoretical theories.

Using the DSM III-R, clients are rated on five independent dimensions or axes as follows:

Axis I. Clinical syndrome — current episode of the illness, more florid symptoms

Axis II. Personality disorder — frequently overlooked long term disturbance, or underlying disorder, or personality trait

Axis III. Physical disorder or condition

Axis IV. Severity of psycho-social stressors (rated on a scale from 1 (none) to 7 (catastrophic)

Axis V. Highest level of adaptive functioning within the past year (including the three dimensions of social relations, occupational functioning, and leisure time) using a composite scale from 1 (superior) to 5 (poor).

All these serve as guidelines in arriving at a differential diagnosis and are considered in detecting individual disorders and in planning appropriate intervention.

Because discrimination among diagnoses is challenging and difficult, for each disorder the description in the DSM III-R contains a list of essential features of that disorder. It also offers a clinical sketch, based upon a summary of characteristics, information about the typical onset and course of the disorder, and predisposing factors. Frequency of occurrence, and information on similar disorders is also provided. A disorder is conceptualized as a clinically significant behavioral or psychological syndrome or pattern that occurs in an individual that is typically associated with either a painful symptom in one or more important areas of functioning.

One can clearly see in this latest edition of the DSM, absent from the preceding editions, an attempt to broaden the diagnostic configuration to include physical, environmental and functional measurements.

DSM III-R takes a phenomenological, descriptive approach rather than an etiological and theoretical one. Its purpose is to determine the presence or absence of identified features in order to arrive at a coded assessment or diagnosis.

Supporters of this assessment system for psycho-social problems consider it to be pragmatic and empirical, classifying symptoms that develop a clinical picture that is understandable by other clinicians, leading to an effective treatment plan. A common misconception is that individuals are being classified. What actually is being classified or labeled are disorders that individuals have. For this reason, the DSM III-R avoids the use of such labels as "an alcoholic" or "a schizophrenic." Refinement in multiaxial classification is offered by decision trees designed to discriminate among various symptoms. The aim of the DSM is (1) promoting elegance in diagnosis for clinicians while simultaneously (2) improving better communication between and among the different mental health disciplines and (3) serving as a valuable tool for teaching about psychopathology and mental illness.

Problems can arise from using the DSM III-R because it involves a labeling process in which clients become identified with stereotypic attitudes and beliefs associated with the label. This, in turn, as discussed in Chapter VI, shapes the way others interact with clients and negatively influences the clients' self-perception. A pattern of self-fulfilling expectation may hinder rather than enhance resolution of problems or relief from symptoms. Critics claim that few clients exactly fit DSM categories, criteria are vague and discrete treatment is not indicated for specified conditions. The DSM III-R is criticized as being a limited and crude but all too popular method of labeling disease which contributes little of practical value in terms of prognosis and treatment. It deals scantily with clients' inner world and does not deal with deepened understanding of clients' strengths and aspirations. It does not add, but, rather, removes information; it does not present a full picture and may deceive clinicians into believing that they have uncovered some particular entity, a disorder, instead of focusing on the full range of client attributes.

Advocates of the DSM III-R claim that although it has limitations, it is a clear and consistent system of classification which provides the first step of help to clients. They argue that it provides structure and organization which serves as a shorthand for communication among professional colleagues.

The DSM III-R can be instructive and helpful when you are mindful of its limitations, and use it selectively and with discretion.

The DSM III-R Assessment of Elaine

According to the DSM III-R, Elaine would be assessed as having a mood disorder. More specifically, she would be labeled as having a Dysthymic Disorder (300.40). She presented the affective picture of being sad, dull, tired with self-debasement; the intellectual picture of uncertainty and self-reproach; and the physical picture of loss of sleep and restlessness for at least a two year period, she had never had either a manic episode or psychotic delusions. When examined medically, no organic or chemical imbalance was found that contributed to or maintained her disturbance. Earlier Major Depressive symptoms from her teen years were in complete remission. There was no suicidal ideation at the present moment. Axis III would indicate no physical disorder or condition. The severity of psycho-social stressors, Axis IV, would be approximately 6, with particular consideration to enduring circumstances in her life (e.g., family factors), in concert with acute events (occupational and living circumstances). Axis V, highest level of adaptive functioning with the past year, was rated at 3, indicating that her functioning was fair or adequate.

OTHER DIMENSIONS IN ASSESSMENT

There are a number of other factors that need to be taken into account when assessing individual clients. These factors apply as well to making an assessment of family functioning.

These factors include:

— availability of friends and family,
— characteristics of clients' residence
— illnesses and accidents
— ethnic, religious and cultural factors
— **clients' physical constitution and health**
— temperamental elements.

AN INTEGRATED APPROACH

To achieve a synthesis that brings together the available components of the person and the situation in an orderly and economic manner which permits comprehensive assessment and responsible decisions about intervention, you need to consider many variables. These variables include an evaluation of clients' past efforts at resolution of the identified problem, reasons for not resolving it, and current and past precipitants. The style in which clients address problem solving; their motivation; agreement or disparity between behavior and related feeling; degree of fear and affective appropriateness are of vital importance.

Recognize the defenses clients employ and the extent to which they are used, their capacity to deal with feelings as well as reality issues and the nature and quality of their response to you. Additional factors to consider in client appraisal are their intellectual functioning, judgment, self-concept, functional beliefs, misconceptions, dynamic interaction between cognition, emotions and behavior, and range of emotions.

You learn all this by both direct and indirect means. Direct means include questioning, and using existing reports, differential use of diaries, logs, histories, inventories, family trees, and spontaneous self-reports. Indirect means involve observation of behavior in the interview with you, body language, tone of voice and correspondence between what clients say and the way they show affect.

In order to help you distinguish whether clients experience disturbances of feeling, thought, behavior, social relationships, work or school performance, physical function, and to appraise the degree of severity or dysfunction in themselves or in the environment, pay close attention to their appearance, posture, facial expressions and general body movements. Ask yourself these questions: What is the state of clients' general physical tension? Are they hyper- or hypoactive? Is anxiety expressed mostly through behavior or words? What is the quality of their relationships? Are clients domineering, submissive, suspicious, cooperative, withdrawn or aggressive? To what extent do the clients' efforts at controlling or concealing emotions succeed? Do they try to evoke pity? Fear? Anger? Other questions include: How accurate are clients' perceptions? What is the content and abstractness of their thinking? What is the quality of their insight, judgment, and memory? How intact are their physical functions — sleep, eating, tics, spasms, seizures, etc? How autonomous are they? What are their attitudes toward themselves? Is there environmental mastery? Adequacy in interpersonal relationships? How do they meet situational requirements and social pressures? Is there evidence of environmentally created problems or stress? Are there available resources? What are their talents and skills? What is their education and work history?

An Integrated Perspective on Elaine

No one school or approach has a monopoly on assessment or interventive effectiveness. The following evaluation shows how a variety of theories and techniques were blended in individual work with Elaine. Chapter VIII details how individual work was complemented by a family systems approach.

Work with Elaine concentrated first on initial expression of feelings of sadness, low personal worth, incompetence and failure and on catharsis, releasing energy from bringing repressed or forgotten material into awareness. Discussion and examination of recent relationships showed a pattern of arriving at unsatisfactory and premature solutions to problems by sacrificing her own feelings, as she had done as a child to win parental approval. As a consequence she often felt resentful. The resentment was subsequently self-directed.

During our initial contacts, Elaine was unable to extract even a minute sense of achievement or progress in the work; indeed, for a while, the more she uncovered and felt, the more contemptible she felt. I encouraged Elaine to talk more with the friends she had and to develop some alliances with support systems — colleagues, and fellow craftspeople.

Early individual work also drew upon a cognitive/behavioral perspective. Attention was directed at correcting Elaine's perception of being unable to survive and satisfy her own needs. We collaborated to examine how her style of thinking contributed to sustaining her depressive mood. She "sensed" that she had "somehow" acquired the negative concept of herself through harsh judgments by and identification with key family and religious figures in her life. She could be no more explicit about this "sense."

Elaine's own negative judgments reinforced a self-concept of being "bad." To compensate, she set extremely high expectations for herself and then judged her inevitably poor performance by these unreasonable standards. She came to recognize how such a cycle crystallized a pattern for ongoing negative attitudes which eventually became entrenched. Elaine was especially receptive to the process of monitoring her automatic negative thinking, examining the inter-connection between her thinking, feeling and behavior, and continually resorting to processes of overgeneralization and self-devaluation. I assigned homework directed at her recalling and jotting down on index cards any present or childhood accomplishments which surfaced misconceptions about her abilities into active awareness. Stimulated by her intellectual recognition of achievements—academic awards in school, excellent employment evaluations and promotions, prizewinning crafts, and by getting a grip on her emotions, she began to experiment with changing dysfunctional beliefs and perceiving herself more realistically. She substituted more reality-oriented thinking about her accomplishments and her self. Her depressed mood and paralysis of will lifted.

Successive successful experiences using cognitive and behavioral methods, bolstered by acknowledgement of her educational, occupational and personal achievements, despite apparent trauma in her past, led Elaine to be able to express her feelings more completely and to grant herself permission to make mistakes. She became increasingly self-assertive. Elaine began to come to terms with the distortion between her image of herself and objective facts.

Throughout our contact, gestalt experiments and dramatization techniques were employed to slow her down and connect her more fully with internal affects. They also kept her in touch with the details of her experience. Such experiments brought into the foreground Elaine's avoided feelings. They were successful in getting her to acknowledge, accept and support herself and to contact and confront concealed memories and emotions from her past. It was still very difficult, however, for her to overcome blocks to seeing the missing pieces, details or "holes," in her early experience.

As described extensively in Chapter X, through the added use of the log, and the childhood diaries she supplied from her early teen years, her memory gradually improved about early childhood events. This phase of the work resurfaced reminiscences of episodes of early childhood conflict. She became more amenable to intensive and active exploration of dim memories and associations leading to her understanding the impact that hurts, difficulties and defeats in childhood had on her present functioning. Interpretation of her relationship with me, an authoritarian male who did not degrade, abuse or manipulate her for his own purposes, as did other men in the past, enabled her not only to gain insight into her self-defeating cycle that resulted in inescapable feelings of shame, but also allowed her to draw upon her creative energy to confront these feelings and behave differently. Increased awareness of previously hidden aspects, when considered in historical context, enabled her to risk breaking a repetitive pattern of expecting to be treated badly and almost ritually behaving in a way to ensure its happening.

As Elaine's view of herself, the helping process, and her immediate present context became more realistic, she felt more positive, trusting and hopeful, and her sense of guilt, shame, and failure diminished. Earning money from craftwork, making friends and socializing with other volunteers at the Red Cross, obtaining a higher title and salary increase at a new job, all increased her sense of competence and supported the helping process over time aimed at helping her muster and accept these gains. Her ambivalence was greatly reduced. As blocks to recollection of her family faded, she was encouraged to deal directly with her family which furthered her progress.

Integrated "S's"

The following summary, "10 S's" is one I use as a guide in assessing individuals. It attempts to integrate pertinent components from the Psychodynamic, Existential, Behavioral as well as other models.

1. Situational variables — culture, socio-economic conditions
2. Symptoms
3. Structure of personality — especially ego functions of perception, memory, reasoning and problem solving

4. Sense of self—esteem, integration, spontaneity
5. Strengths—adaptation, achievements, resilience
6. Solutions sought
7. Sources of conflict
8. Separateness—differentiation, individuation
9. Synthesis of behavior, affect, and thinking
10. Systems variables—family context, social and environmental supports.

The following chapter describes how a family orientation enhanced Elaine's progress and development in a positive direction.

REFERENCES

Alexander, Franz. *Psychoanalysis and Psychotherapy.* NY: Norton, 1956.

Bandura, A. *Principles of Behavior Modification.* NY: Holt, Rinehart and Winston, 1969.

Bandura, A. *Social Foundations of Thought and Action.* Englewood Cliffs, NJ: 1986.

Brenner, Charles. *An Elementary Textbook of Psychoanalysis.* NY: International Universities Press, 1973.

Bugental, James. *The Search for Existential Identity.* San Francisco: Jossey-Bass, 1976.

Diagnostic and Statistical Manual of Mental Disorders (3rd Edition). Washington, DC: American Psychiatric Association, 1987.

Fenichel, Otto. *The Psychoanalytic Theory of Neurosis.* NY: Norton, 1945.

Frankl, Victor. *Man's Search for Meaning.* NY: Basic Books, 1963.

Frankl, Victor. *Will to Meaning.* NY: World Publishing, 1969.

Freud, Anna. *The Ego and the Mechanisms of Defense.* NY: International Universities Press, 1966.

Freud, Sigmund. *Introductory Lectures on Psychoanalysis.* London: Hogarth Press, 1915-17.

Fromm, Eric. *Escape from Freedom.* NY: Rinehart and Winston, 1941.

Hall, Calvin. *A Primer of Freudian Psychology.* NY: New American Library, 1973.

Hartmann, Heinz. *Essays on Ego Psychology.* NY: International Universities Press, 1964.

Lazarus, Arnold. *Behavior Therapy and Beyond.* NY: McGraw-Hill, 1971.

Lazarus, Arnold. *The Practice of Multimodal Therapy.* NY: McGraw-Hill, 1981.

May, Rollo. *Freedom and Destiny.* NY: Norton, 1981.

May, Rollo. *Love and Will.* NY: Norton, 1969.

May, Rollo. *The Meaning of Anxiety.* NY: Norton, 1977.
O'Leary, K. D. et al., *Behavior Therapy: Application and Outcome (2nd Ed.).* Englewood Cliffs, N.J.: Prentice-Hall, 1987.
Shapiro, David. *Neurotic Styles.* NY: Basic Books, 1965.
Wolpe, J. *The Practice of Behavior Therapy.* NY: Pergamon Press, 1969.
Yalom, Irving. *Existential Psychotherapy.* NY: Basic Books, 1981.

Chapter VIII

Models of Helping: Working with a Family

Everything in this universe is linked to everything else.

—John Muir

As you ought not to attempt to cure the eyes without the head, or the head without the body, so neither ought you to attempt to cure the body without the soul . . . the whole . . . ought to be studied also; for the part can never be well unless the whole is well.

—Plato, CHARMIDES

The traditional approaches to assessment and intervention, as outlined in the previous chapter, view symptoms as expressions of conflict within individuals (Psychodynamic theory), between individuals and "givens" in life (Existential theory), and between individuals and their environment (Behavioral theory). This chapter presents another viewpoint derived from family systems theory. It demonstrates how a combined systems and individual approach complement and enrich each other. When, in your practice, you take a comprehensive view of clients' functioning and integrate methods of assessment and intervention from individual and family schools, therapy is deepened and change is hastened.

Family systems theory views symptoms as evolving from within family contexts. The emphasis, therefore, in family systems assessment and intervention is on interactional and relational patterns rather than on intrapsychic or individual dilemmas. Problems are seen as emerging as a consequence of families' failure to accommodate to the developmental needs of individuals and to transitions in families' life cycles.

Often, as in Elaine's family, discussed below, when distressful symptoms manifest themselves in one individual, other family members are saved from facing severe anxieties. Ordinarily, if families come to understand the value of the symptoms, they can let go of them.

Elaine's story, introduced in Chapter VII, is developed further in this chapter from a family systems perspective. The usual process of engaging the entire family to participate in such a formal process of intervention was not possible. What was possible, however, was to utilize a family systems orientation to help Elaine come to terms with her depression. I introduced a broader scope of assessment strategies in relation to her family context. She was willing to re-enter her family to undertake structured and rehearsed contacts making it possible to evaluate comprehensively Elaine's depressive symptoms and to intervene more effectively to alter her maladaptive patterns.

ELAINE'S FAMILY

Elaine progressed well in her individual work as described in Chapter VII. She became more comfortable with the helping process and recognized that it helped her to sort out problems. She felt relief from much of her distress. As she perused her logs with me, she became willing to take a closer look at her family. At first she resisted doing so, seeing it as disloyal. However, after experiencing some success from rehearsed scheduled visits home with prescribed tasks, she became increasingly absorbed in family exploration.

Elaine's logs, filled with a raging mixture of thoughts and feelings, gave both of us data clearly showing a disturbed family system and indicating how she responded to it. The logs revealed also how she maintained the very system that oppressed her.

For Elaine, everyone elses' wants and needs had precedence over her own. Her family and her religion taught her to be all sacrificing, all giving, all loving. It also taught her to have no expectations for herself, to make no requests. She remembers her father often commenting, "You're a nobody, Elaine." One particularly vivid memory of his saying this was after she had refused to enter a psychiatric hospital for her own acute depression because she felt obliged to take care of her sister, who had broken her leg. In effect, anything anyone wanted her to be or to do, came first. Her compliance rebounded and further contributed to her self-contempt. She felt that she had abdicated her personhood. No boundaries existed between her, her parents, and her siblings.

Elaine reflected that even as a child she did not often think or act as a child. She certainly never felt like one. She recalled being criticized by her mother for "never being a child." She also heard the explicit message from her mother—no-one would ever like her.

To make herself feel better, and to feel more accepted by the family, she dissolved herself. She accommodated to everyone's whims. Even when she lived with her maternal grandparents, away from home, she felt "pulled" back home. Once home, however, she was miserable and wanted to escape, feeling that her life "would be sucked out" of her. This made her feel guilty and shameful. Religious tenets and family lessons fed her already intense sense of guilt.

Elaine remembered her mother as always being in bed, crying or complaining. She was never available and always demanding. Elaine said that she felt like a shadow who stole into her mother's room to give her some unidentified liquid, for "medicinal purposes." She remembered her father as a church elder who violated every rule he preached and imposed upon her. He secretly drank and "womanized." Abandoned by her mother, she was violated by her father. She dispassionately reported vague recollections of incest by her father and by his brother.

Elaine learned early to anesthetize herself. The few memories she had of interaction between her parents involved her father berating her mother for being "lazy" and "sick," and her mother screaming at her father about his drinking and his affairs. Both of her parents tried to enlist her to side with them in their arguments. Feeling helpless about stopping them, she saw herself as inadequate and defective. Indeed, she came to see herself as causing the family's problem. She seemed to punish herself for not having "saved" her family.

Elaine's siblings conspired with her view of causing the family problems. They constantly let her know that they were distressed by her presence. They either joined in their parents' mocking her, or ignored her completely. Her older brother, who disappeared when he was seventeen, resented her entirely and would not even talk to her. Her two younger siblings avoided her except for when they needed her.

Elaine allowed herself to be manipulated and "used" only to end up feeling rejected, disliked and abused. She could not say "No!" Feeling more comfortable in belittling situations, she almost automatically fashioned new relationships in ways to resemble the home she tried to "cut-off."

The second of four children, Elaine was born within a year of her brother's birth. It appeared to have been a time when her parents were having serious marital discord. She was the most vulnerable to increases in family anxiety and was the most poorly differentiated, and most emotionally-fused child. She became the "symptom bearer."

From discussion and reflection on her visits home, and with repeated interpretations based upon assignments dealing first with taking a back seat while at home to eventually taking an active proactive role in stepping out of familial patterns, she recognized that while she was a product of the family interaction, she had also contributed to shaping it. She was able to reshape it now.

Obedience, rigidity and denial of feelings were highly valued in Elaine's family. Even though she sacrificed her feelings to win their approval, they disparaged her.

Elaine's parents' marriage was a vacuum. Her mother was mentally ill and unavailable. Her father was cruelly authoritative and physically and sexually abusive. A spiritually disciplined life was touted as the only one worth living. The trouble was no one actually lived it. Instead, hypocrisy, verbal and physical abuse, and incest dominated the family picture. Elaine was exquisitely responsive to its emotional tumult and hypervigilant in all relationships. She felt torn and guilty for whatever she did although she was eternally loyal, and supremely responsible to her family.

THREE THEORETICAL CONTRIBUTIONS

Freud was the original family therapist. He postulated the central importance of the family in the formation of individual personality. His methods of intervention, however, were retrospective. Acknowledging the central input of family interaction, he and his followers focused on internalized figures or events from the past as recollected in the present. Contemporary family therapists (Napier and Whitaker, Framo, Haley, Minuchin, Madanes, and Satir) focus on current ongoing experiences of families and intervene directly to disrupt and alter dysfunctions.

Whatever your theoretical or methodological preference, it is important to recognize that individuals originate from and live in families and that families are composed of individuals, each with a separate history. As Toman said,

> Since family contexts are among an individual's oldest life contexts, since they are the most regularly effective, longest-lasting, contexts stemming from the individual's earliest years, we may assume that generalizations and transferences from them to new social situations are likely to have occurred more often and may have influenced the perception and even the active shaping of contemporary life contexts more strongly than those life contexts that the individual has experienced only later in his life. (Toman, 1976, 77)

Take account of families' past and present influence on clients. Work to have clients understand their subjective worlds and internalized images, as well as actively interconnect with available family members to break fragile and binding chains or to strengthen or create healthy links.

The brief abstracts below of three major family approaches— Psychoanalytic, Structural and Intergenerational, show how each conceptualizes family assessment and intervention. As in Chapter VII, Elaine's story is featured to exemplify how these theories are applied in practice. The theory of family assessment and intervention is not as codified as that of individual assessment and intervention; therefore these abstracts, samples of an ever expanding assortment of family systems approaches, are merely suggestive representations of the broad range of possible ways to conceptualize family assessment and intervention. The newness and explosion of differing conceptualizations make it impossible to develop encapsulations similar to those offered above for assessing individuals. I present my own guide for assessing families which is organized into a list of 10 "A's." It represents my attempt to integrate these three theories, together with contributions from the Strategic and Family Life Cycle frames of reference.

THE PSYCHOANALYTIC PERSPECTIVE ON THE FAMILY

The psychoanalytic approach to family assessment and intervention (Ackerman, Boszormenyi-Nagy, Framo, Zuk) stresses unconscious interactions among family members. Spouses bring impairments, residues from unresolved conflicts with their own families of origin, which are unconsciously re-enacted in the present with other members of the family. Partners unwittingly select each other out of self-destructive patterns learned in their own families. Their unrecognized and repressed needs lead them to coerce each other and their children repeatedly and compulsively re-enact past scenarios.

Spouses get absorbed in a process called projective identification, a process in which disowned aspects of parents' personalities are projected onto each other or onto their children and then are reacted to accordingly. Clients' functioning in the family is seen, in other words, largely as a consequence of remnants of parental relationships which they spontaneously relive with spouses and children. Louis' and Harriet's marriage is one example of this phenomenon.

Louis, born in Puerto Rico, was raised single-handedly from infancy by his mother. His father had abandoned his mother before Louis was born. Shy and withdrawn as a child, he would hide in a closet whenever his mother entertained male friends because it was the only way he felt safe and comfortable. He would avoid his mother afterwards; in fact the more she tried to get close to him the further away he moved.

Harriet, from Indiana, was youngest of three sisters. Her father was emotionally cold and physically distant. Her mother was repeatedly hospitalized for schizophrenia. To feel warmth and comforted, Harriet remembered literally crawling to the house next door where, encouraged by her neighbor, she would repeatedly lick her finger, dip it into the sugar bowl and lick it again.

Louis and Harriet had trouble from the earliest years of their marriage. They were unable to get from each other the type of attention and affection they wanted. When Harriet felt alone and insecure, she would flood Louis with demands for verbal and physical reassurances of his love. Louis' response would be to withdraw further away from her. Harriet, panicked by his "rejection," increased her demands. Louis, overwhelmed by her needs, distanced himself even further. Blind to their underlying feelings and motives, they both felt trapped and unloved.

The task of a psychoanalytically-oriented family therapist is to reactivate and decode the hidden meaning behind clients' repetitious cycles, like those illustrated by Louis and Harriet, and free them to interact with one another on the basis of current realities rather than images from the past.

Problems are viewed as a function of individuals' personalities which are manifested in the interaction among family members. They develop from compromises intended to meet suppressed needs and avoid threatening members. Having to face the stress of life transitions for which they are unprepared, families resort to earlier or more primitive and unproductive ways of interacting. Unconscious forces, then, propel the family into dysfunctional and maladaptive patterns. Since spontaneous interactions, occurring unavoidably even in the presence of the helper, manifest covert motives, assessment entails penetrating beneath the surface in a non-directive, neutral way. It emphasizes reducing families' defensiveness, and, thereby, giving them access to hidden causes of problem interaction. This understanding fosters change.

The chief tool of assessment and change in the psychoanalytic family perspective is to facilitate the emergence of forgotten and avoided feelings and relationship patterns. Objective recognition and interpretation of these leads to insight into how parents inadvertently but inevitably repeat their own idiosyncratic pasts between themselves and with their children. This insight, combined with analysis of how their defenses operate in dealing with needs and feelings where the present is misjudged in terms of the past, ultimately encourages and instructs families to continue on their own with the uncovering process. The goal of intervention is not merely the elimination of symptoms. It is also discovery of secret meanings and termination of troublesome cycles of interaction.

A Psychoanalytic Perspective on Elaine's Family

The scanty information provided by Elaine about her parents' backgrounds in her logs, in her reminiscences, and in her genogram suggested unconscious and conflictual residues from their own pasts which they reenacted with each other and their children with dire consequences. Her family continually evoked dysfunctional defenses, including isolation, rationalization, projection, and denial, to avoid being overwhelmed by intrapsychic and interpersonal anxiety and to maintain equilibrium in the face of threatening events. Their unresolved inner lives and conflicts interlocked with each other and bound them together to form and perpetuate disturbances. In other words, they visited onto their children their own "stuckness." Deeper emotional currents of fear, suspicion, urge for vengeance and power were rampant.

THE STRUCTURAL PERSPECTIVE
ON THE FAMILY

Structuralists, such as Aponte, Haley, Minuchin, hold that problems in family functioning arise from a failure of families to adapt to changing circumstances. Individual symptoms are viewed as by-products of this problem. Individuals' symptomatic behavior and distorted sense of reality results from families' governing, but maladaptive, superstructures. Superstructures are sets or sums of unstated rules of interaction which determine the behavior patterns and organize the view of reality, not only of the family system as a whole, but also of the individuals who comprise it.

Assessment requires attending to families' boundaries and structure, which, because they tend to be rigid, lead to repetitive and predictable patterns of interaction. Referred to by Minuchin as "isomorphs," these patterns can be elicited, deliberately and selectively, in the helping process. When they are elicited in this way, they can be renegotiated and modified. Attention is particularly directed at the "executive system," the parental subsystem, and how it functions. Parents are encouraged to form an alliance with each other, rather than with their children, and to treat children age-appropriately — not made either too powerful or too subjugated. Assessment is called "mapping," illustrated later in the case of Elaine, which identifies over-flexibility or over-rigidity of roles, rules and familial alignments. It takes measure of families' flexibility, richness and coherence of functioning patterns; resonance or degree of enmeshment or disengagement; life context, sources of support and stress; developmental stage; and function of the individuals' presenting symptoms as protective, defensive, or conflictual.

"Mapping" is an experiential diagnosis of family functioning based upon observation of family interaction either spontaneously or at your provocation. It conceptualizes the complex organizational system, ecological context and developmental stage on paper by means of a symbolic diagram. The schematic in Figure 8 shows some of the symbols used in structural "mapping."

The aim of structural intervention, unlike psychoanalytic intervention, is symptom resolution through recognizing and reorganizing the particular dysfunctional part of families' interdependent structure. Focusing on the immediate in-session behavior, only secondary attention is paid to awareness and historical material. "Dynamics" are not interpreted.

A number of techniques are employed for assessment and intervention — "joining" or becoming part of the family system in order to experience its world view and to redirect its interaction into more functional channels; escalating stress by re-arranging seats, giving tasks, commands and directions, and excluding certain members. Direct techniques include blocking communication, confronting individuals to speak for themselves and challenging family myths.

FIGURE 8. Symbols for Mapping Family Structure

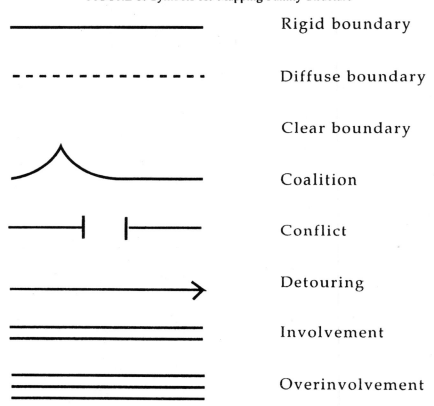

Rigid boundary

Diffuse boundary

Clear boundary

Coalition

Conflict

Detouring

Involvement

Overinvolvement

Offering metaphors, reframing and challenging belief systems are some indirect techniques that are used. These techniques are intended to modify the communication and relational system and reform the families' dysfunctional hierarchies, boundaries, alignments and power structure.

A Structural Perspective on Elaine's Family

Elaine's family's rigid hierarchical structure and lack of clear boundaries maintained negative feedback cycles that trapped Elaine into an overly responsible role as caretaker not only of her siblings,

but of her parents as well. The patterns of defeat, misplaced authority, and inflexible rules were supported and sustained by the family's strict religious and social context. The "map" in Figure 9
diagrams the family's entrenched framework, intruding on Elaine's
space and resulting in a parental role for Elaine, even as a child.

THE INTERGENERATIONAL PERSPECTIVE
ON THE FAMILY

According to Intergeneration theory (Bowen, Guerin, Kerr and
Bowen, McGoldrick and Gerson) individuals' self-image and
chronic anxiety are formed in reaction to the anxieties and emotional
neediness of parents who define their children through their own
distorted perceptions. Pressure is applied to children to make them
conform to established regimens in order to be rewarded with acceptance and approval.

This approach best interfaces with individual approaches. It
encourages approaching family of origin members to facilitate a
rapprochement with meaningful others in their lives. More importantly, it seeks actual contact with other family members themselves.

Bowen, the most prominent theoretician of this school, identifies
four ways in which families deal with anxiety and tension: (1) increased emotional distance between spouses; (2) physical or emotional dysfunction in a spouse; (3) overt, repeated, but unresolved
marital conflict; and (4) impairment in a child. Bowen, in assessing
families, takes a close look at sibling position, and multi-generation
transmission of anxiety. Since there is a basic emotional connectedness between the generations that results in each generation having
a significant influence on the emotional process in the generation
that follows, family projection, nuclear emotional systems, triangles and individual differentiation are critical elements to be addressed. Family projection occurs when immature parents create
dysfunction in one or more of their children. The nuclear family
emotional system refers to the way a family in a single generation
controls fusion, "stuck-togetherness," or unresolved emotional parental attachment. The ways in which people manage the intensity
of emotional attachments is through triangles. A two person rela-

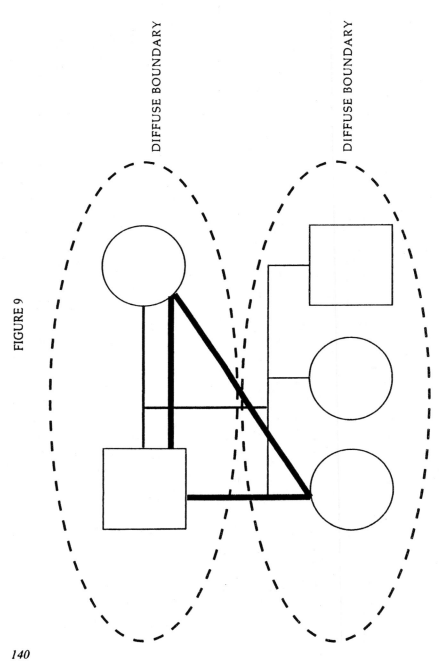

FIGURE 9

DIFFUSE BOUNDARY

DIFFUSE BOUNDARY

tionship has a low tolerance for anxiety and is easily disturbed by emotional forces within the couple or in the environment. As anxiety increases, the emotional flow in the couple correspondingly intensifies and the relationship becomes uncomfortable. When it becomes oppressive, the couple involve a vulnerable third person, usually a child. The involvement of the third person, who forms the triangle, reduces the anxiety level. "Differentiation" describes clients' capacity to be aware of the difference between their intellectual and their emotionally determined functioning in relationships, and to have some choice about the degree to which each type governs their behavior.

The principal tool for conducting an assessment is the genogram. The genogram is used methodically throughout the helping endeavor, to assess all the patterns mentioned above. Unlike Structuralists, Intergenerationalists do not "join" the family; rather, remaining calm, rational, and dispassionate they stay "outside" families' emotional and projection system in order to make rationally sound, objective appraisals of functioning.

Intervention, based on assessment, involves redefining individuals in relation to the balance of separateness and connectedness and reopening cut-off family relationships. In addition to developing a genogram, homework tasks, usually involving contact with a wide spectrum of family members, are prescribed to enhance assessment by providing opportunity for firsthand observation by the clinician and, ultimately, by the family members themselves, of functioning. In this manner, families' mythology and pressures placed on individuals to conform to dysfunctional patterns are exposed, reduced, and redirected. This approach relies strongly on planned systematic techniques of non-confrontation and non-defensive re-working of relationships to change individuals' position in their families. The change in position forces families to adjust to these changes.

Intergenerationalists postulate that effective work is contingent upon your ability as a helper to look at, understand and come to terms with the emotional functioning of your own family of origin. If you do not, you can unknowingly become "triangulated" into the conflict of the families with whom you work.

The Genogram

The genogram, an innovation of Intergenerational theorists and practitioners in family treatment, captures information about family members in graphic form. Data include their location and significant dates — births, marriages, deaths. The genogram helps assess the legacy of families' unique milieu and patterns which played a significant part in the development of symptoms expressed by individual members. A graphic representation of families' structure and fabric, the genogram captures the details of at least three generations in a formal way. It provides a roadmap of relationships, patterns of closeness, boundaries, operating principles and conflictual issues. It offers a glimpse at the characteristics of the extended family and red-flags pivotal issues. Attending to incidental information, as the genogram is developed and discussed, gives clues that reveal central themes. These themes, in turn, become a rich source of hypotheses leading to solutions as well as to a better picture of problems.

The genogram opens up issues that have long been *taboo*, fostering an exploration of emotionally charged issues and suggesting alternative strategies. Family members' reactions during construction of the genogram reflect the private world of families' idiosyncratic characteristics. It can be utilized effectively in work with individuals, couples, or whole families. A schematic of the basic three generation genogram is illustrated in Figure 10, and the symbols used to construct genograms are shown in Figure 11.

An Intergenerational Perspective on Elaine's Family

Elaine was caught in an overclose relationship with her parents in which all played on each other's fears and fantasies. She was programmed into the spousal pair to dilute their anxiety. The stability Elaine brought to the marital pair made it possible for them to tolerate each other, but at a price — Elaine's fusion. Projected onto her was the fallout of the parallel position each of her parents sustained as second, "replaced," undifferentiated children each in their own respective families of origin. As the most emotionally bound child, she had the lowest level of differentiation and the highest level of difficulty in separating. The irony was that her identity was associ-

FIGURE 10. Basic Three Genogram

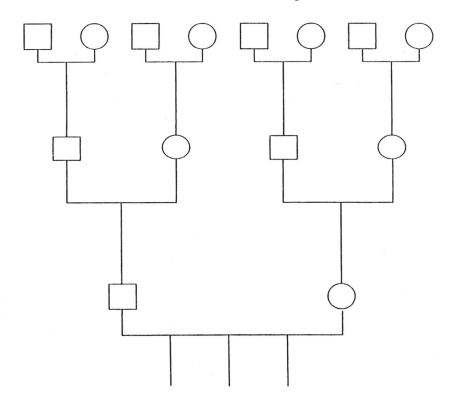

ated with this closeness. She had to "cut-off" to escape and mask her attachment even from herself.

The genogram of Elaine's family depicts cross-generational emotional cut-offs, triangles, and patterns of interpersonal conflict between siblings and parents and similarly positioned children. Because the family would not cooperate in the helping process, it was impossible to precisely corroborate data. Nonetheless, even from Elaine's uni-dimensional and biased perspective, it seemed evident that the serious psychosocial stresses of the family were exacerbated by drugs, alcohol and chronic infidelity.

FIGURE 11. Genogram Symbols

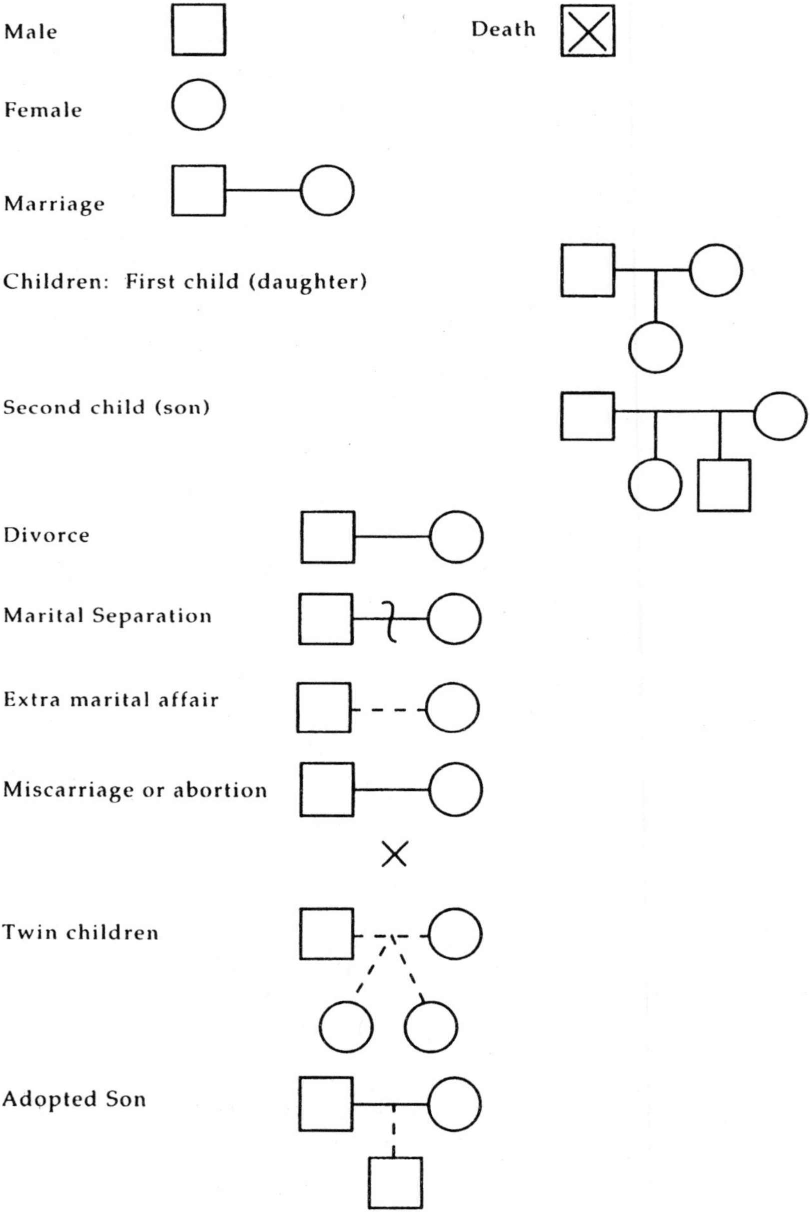

Male

Death

Female

Marriage

Children: First child (daughter)

Second child (son)

Divorce

Marital Separation

Extra marital affair

Miscarriage or abortion

Twin children

Adopted Son

COMMON ELEMENTS IN FAMILY APPROACHES

While different in many ways in their conceptualizations of family assessment and intervention, there are elements that most theoretical approaches to families share in common. These elements distinguish them from strictly individually oriented frameworks for practice. These common elements are:

- Belief that change emanates from the context of family interaction rather than from individual intrapsychic factors
- Emphasis on conscious communication rather than unconscious, covert processes
- Engagement of the whole family in the helping process
- Utilization of crises and confrontations
- Stress on recognizing present functioning, not recollecting past events
- De-emphasis of insight and understanding; concentration on behavioral change.

When working from a family orientation, pay close attention to subtle and marginal clues produced by families in their interaction during sessions. Keep in mind such questions as: Who talks to whom? Under what circumstances? What makes the family tick? What are the alliances? What are the dilemmas? How do they function? and How can they move to a higher level of functioning?

Assessment and intervention go hand in hand. Family assessment also devotes attention to families' developmental stages, described differently by different theorists, as they progress from commitment through parenting to old age and retirement.

AN INTEGRATED PERSPECTIVE ON ELAINE'S FAMILY

It is not possible for any one method or technique alone to provide complete and definite resolution of such complex problems as those presented by Elaine. Over-exercising one specialized approach often leads to tunnel vision and restricted interaction; likewise, rigid adherence to one method often leads to being close but just off center enough to miss by a mile. Integration of differing approaches offers the most solid base for family intervention. Work with Elaine, therefore, drew from both individual and family theories and relied upon a number of different, although interdependent, techniques. Adjustments were made in the intervention to accommodate to the changing assessment, which, in turn, was influenced by effective interventions. Every attempt was made not to fit Elaine to a modality, but, instead, to fit the assessment and intervention to her individual and family dynamics and requirements.

Particularly because she felt even more rejected by her family's refusal to cooperate with her in the work, meeting her need for support while not interfering with her autonomous ego functions helped to thaw-out her frozen views and patterns. It provided a cushion to her feeling totally misunderstood and isolated. This was accompanied by attempts to make sense out of the family's influence to complement the progress Elaine made in the initial individual work.

Elaine had geographically cut herself off from her family in an attempt to differentiate herself. She was not successful in this because she remained emotionally glued to it. She agreed to ask her family to join her periodically for a marathon meeting with an inducement to visit the "Big Apple." Although they took her up on her offer to come to New York, all flatly refused to participate in family sessions. This did not stop us from assuming a family orientation.

Elaine was encouraged to take an observer, "researcher" position regarding her own family. Work proceeded along two complementary lines. The first was the construction of the genogram of her family, over an extended period of time, which prompted new ways of thinking about and being with her parents, siblings, and friends. The second built upon the increased self-awareness and enhanced concept of her family to help her re-establish contact, at first by phone and then in person with peripheral members of her family and ultimately with her parents themselves. Woven into the process was her willingness to take an "I" position in her contacts, much like the one she employed in individual sessions using gestalt techniques.

Taking an observer position made it possible for Elaine truly to separate herself from the family's emotionally consuming "mass," and open up space for obtaining a different view of both her past and her present situation. Tracing the history of her nuclear family and its roots, somewhat disentangled her from its emotional grasp. When she began to see her family as a series of interlocking emotional fields extending back through generations, the way and why of people's behavior toward each other and to her took on new meaning. She came to see that the long-standing, continuing transgenerational patterns of abuse and abandonment were not of her causing. Furthermore, when she remembered episodes of sexual abuse from childhood — and I agreed that they were real — she, for the first time, started to trust her own judgment and stopped succumbing to physical and psychological exploitation by friends and colleagues.

Elaine was asked to recognize times when she was able to do something positive for herself, not to conform to the dominant patterns in her family. This began a counter story of being able to succeed despite having problems. Elaine came to appreciate instances when she performed in a way substantially different from the patterns she previously learned. This generated a self-experience contradicting the original scenario she presented. It provided a new experience and a new map for her.

Before contacting her family, we talked about her expectations to minimize surprises. Elaine contacted her siblings and grandparents at first by letter, then by telephone. She followed these contacts by scheduled brief and coached visits home to her parents. Communicating directly with other family members provided a different and more balanced reality which further challenged the view offered by her parents and siblings. Reconnecting with her parents also released her from her triangled position because she recognized *their* scapegoating, hidden agenda, and lack of boundaries.

Repairing "cut-offs" in small doses on a one-to-one basis, allowed her to come to terms with her parents' imperfection. She found ways to talk directly to each of them. With continual coaching, especially about predicting and preparing for the opposition she would face, Elaine was able to interrupt being automatically sucked back into an unhealthy place. This progress carried over into her relationship with me and with other friends.

The least successful and most dissatisfying aspect of the work involved her siblings. She had no way of reaching her older brother and her contacts with her younger siblings were met with negativity and resistance.

Eventually though, she not only *identified* dysfunctional family rules and codes, Elaine *broke* them. And for the first time, she felt clean.

TEN KEY FACTORS
IN INTEGRATED FAMILY ASSESSMENT
AND INTERVENTION

Following is my attempt to integrate relevant elements from various models into a framework for assessing families. It is formulated into the 10 "A's" of assessment of family functioning. It is intended to complement the 10 "S's" of individual assessment found in Chapter VII:

1. Attributes — special features, distinguishing strengths, remarkable characteristics
2. Abilities — problem solving, coping abilities, competencies
3. Affection — intimacy, caring, need satisfaction
4. Affiliation — belonging, boundaries, splits, alliances
5. Autonomy — differentiation, dependency, stability, developmental stage
6. Arrangement of the infrastructure — triangles, spousal and sibling subsystems, roles, scapegoating
7. Atmosphere — warm, cool, trusting, conflictual, controlled
8. Adaptation to the environment — cultural, religious, social
9. Artifacts — rituals, rules
10. Anomalies — myths, secrets, uniquenesses.

This chapter has emphasized the contribution of family systems thinking to the assessment and intervention processes. Clinical practice is greatly enhanced when a comprehensive approach is employed. Here work with Elaine is traced using a family orientation which adds breadth to individual work. The next chapter elucidates how additional creative techniques were incorporated into clinical work with Elaine and other clients. It presents some new ideas for understanding clients' life stories and ways to integrate these into your clinical practice.

REFERENCES

Ackerman, Nathan. *The Psychodynamics of Family Life*. NY: Basic Books, 1958.

Ackerman, Nathan. *Treating the Troubled Family*. NY: Basic Books, 1966.

Aponte, Harry. "Structural Family Therapy," in Gurman (ed.) *Handbook of Family Therapy*. NY: Brunner/Mazel, 1972.

Aponte, Harry. "Underorganization in the Poor Family," In Guerin (ed.), *Family Therapy*. NY: Gardner Press, 1976.

Bowen, Murray. *Family Therapy in Clinical Practice*. NY: Aronson, 1978.

Boszormenyi-Nagy, Ivan and G. Spark. *Invisible Loyalties*. NY: Harper and Row, 1973.

Framo, James. *Family Interaction*. NY: Springer, 1982.

Guerin, Philip. *Family Therapy*. NY: Gardner Press, 1976.

Haley, Jay. *Leaving Home*. NY: McGraw-Hill, 1980.

Halcy, Jay. *Problem-Solving Therapy*. San Francisco: Jossey-Bass, 1977.

Kerr, Michael and M. Bowen. *Family Evaluation*. NY: Norton, 1988.

McGoldrick, Monica and R. Gerson. *Genograms in Family Assessment*. NY: Norton, 1985.

Madanes, Cloe. *Behind the One-Way Mirror*. San Francisco: Jossey-Bass, 1984.

Minuchin, Salvatore and H. Fishman. *Family Therapy Techniques*. Cambridge, MA: Harvard University Press, 1981.

Minuchin, Salvatore. *Families and Family Therapy*. Cambridge, MA: Harvard University Press, 1974.

Napier, A. and C. Whitaker. *The Family Crucible*. NY: Harper and Row, 1978.

Satir, Virginia. *Conjoint Family Therapy*. Palo Alto, CA: Science and Behavior Books, 1983.

Toman, Walter. *Family Constellation*. NY: Springer, 1976.

Zuk, G. *Process and Practice in Family Therapy*. Haverford, PA: Psychiatry and Behavioral Science Books, 1975.

Zuk, G. *Family Therapy: A Triadic-Based Approach*. NY: Human Sciences Press, 1981.

Chapter IX

Creative Ways of Capturing
the Life Story

For this is the journey that men make: to find themselves. If they fail in this, it doesn't matter much what else they find.

—James Michener

If you have to do it, you might as well enjoy it while you're doing it.

—Milton Erickson

THE LIFE STORY

Your clients' life stories give you and them access to regularities and patterns of being and reacting and give both of you an appreciation of the interconnectedness of all events and responses. When clients tell you their life stories, they are confirming their reality, their existence. Take them seriously. Explore "uneventful" as well as dramatic happenings. Be as fascinated with the ordinary as with the colorful. Seemingly marginal and minimal events reflect the person as much as the outstanding ones do. Often mundane experience opens the door to special drama.

Clients cannot be understood nor understand themselves without knowing something of where they have been. Everything they do relates to everything they have done. It behooves you, therefore, to take full measure of clients' constantly evolving life stories to give meaning and perspective to the helping process. Life stories provide pathways connecting the multiple factors, past and present, that influence clients and serve as a source for discovering something fundamental about their identity. Clients' personal life stories offer you incisive composites of their positive capacities and abilities, a chance to support them further.

The life story is certainly not a set of facts revealing historical truth. It is a narrative that sharply focuses attention on obscure patterns in the client's lives and their construction of reality which helped them make sense out of their lives.

In telling you their life stories, clients reveal the fabric, structure, emotional substance and themes of their lives, adding dimension to your understanding of their special way of processing, integrating and differentiating experience. The aim is not to dig up the past for its own sake, not to reconstruct an exact replica of the past, nor to paint a picture of the past contained in the present. Such an approach would reduce your work to a treasure hunt for past traumatic incidents; indeed, it seems neither possible nor necessarily desirable to do this. If locating original traces is not the aim, what then is the purpose of so close a review of the life stories?

Clients and you access the multifaceted, dynamic interplay among a vast array of factors — maturational, developmental, constitutional and environmental. Examining them puts into perspective the effects of antecedent circumstances, determinants, and traumata on clients' current conflicts and behavioral difficulties. It promotes a far-reaching, and profound portrait of clients' personality, make-up, fears, achievements and disappointments. It helps to ascertain clients' sense of connections between the inner and outer life, the continuity of past, present and future, as well as their transformation capacity — that is, their reaction to disruptions, vicissitudes, conflicts, restrictions and constrictions. It gives a vision of the client's interpretation or misinterpretation of resistance patterns, symptom formation and the ability to change. All of this is seen in light of their future goals, aspirations and dreams. A rich repertoire of affects shaping and modifying clients emerges to distinguish them as unique persons.

Clients shed light on interfamilial dynamics, on the protagonists and antagonists in their lives and on the effect and extent of these influences. In giving you such a closeup of interaction with caretakers, life stories offer a peek at the foundation for the transferential relationship. In brief, life stories supply the tissue that connects and guides your thinking and intervention. They anchor the helping process giving it boundary and direction. They provide you and clients, at the same time, with a greater opportunity to draw upon that knowledge in the change effort.

Because the life story is such an inextricably interwoven composite of ongoing biopsychosocial elements, it is never possible to capture a complete picture of all there is to be known. How, then, can you see clients in the fullest possible way? What makes it possible for you to capture a relatively complete and cohesive picture through the active participation of clients as their own biographical historians? Encouraging them to narrate their life stories in their own way prompts reactivation, recall and a sense of continuity of the life story over time. How clients tell about their intricacies, memories, triumphs and defeats gives access to the actual life drama. How they process the subtleties of omission, discrepancy, distortion and interruption contributes to a greater knowledge of transitions across the life cycle.

As they tell you their life stories, lines of communication open and insight is gained that reverberates within the helping process and in clients' interactions outside the process. Furthermore, the interest you display in the life story is a form of gratification for them which furthers your alliance. Clients' subjective accounts of the life story provide you with a schemata or template of the significant variables in their experience. It helps them to recover and reclaim perhaps long forgotten bits and pieces of their past that were major milestones in their lives.

Clients witness firsthand their distinguishing internal psychic apparatus — temperament, constitution, defenses, drives, juxtaposed against external forces — economic, cultural, religious, that mold and modify them. Life stories highlight the way in which stresses of daily life are handled, a sense of the self-concept and thought processes.

Clients come to understand that they are not at the mercy of random forces, but are able, to a significant extent, to alter their understanding of their histories. It has been pointed out that efforts to **assign context and meaning** to remembered experiences change the face of historical truth (Spence). The evolvement of the life story plumbs deeply and frees understanding; it is a reworking of the life script, and, therefore, promotes healing and provides a new synthesis of the client's biography. Actions, emotions and ideas are continually re-evaluated and reintegrated. It revises the sense of identity, and changes the plot that is vital for continued adaption and maintenance of a cohesive self (Fox). Another way of putting it is to analogize the telling of the life story to replaying "tapes from the past." Replaying tapes from the past makes it possible for clients to edit them, splice sections, add new segments, if not delete or erase portions at least eliminate excessive static or noise, and, overall, create a very different tape.

Clients' life stories, told in their natural language and style, give clues to their internal processes, both conscious and unconscious, of deletion and distortion. Understanding what portions or factors are deleted or distorted improves assessment and guides intervention.

Encouraging clients to tell their life stories is based on a positive expectation of change. It does not envision clients as fixed entities whose form can be analyzed once and for all. It envisions clients as capable of continual revision and refinement and forward movement. Indeed, in the very telling of their life stories, clients alter them.

Significant Elements in the Life Story

We all create stories about the way we are or the way reality is. Drew's story is one illustration.

> Drew, whose mother was distant in childhood, did not like to feel his need for emotional contact because it was too painful and frustrating. He explained his rejection of this need to himself by creating a story he lived by: "Women are not emotionally available. You can never trust them. I will never need a woman."
>
> In relationships with women, Drew would oppose his own need. He would hold back from them emotionally because he never wanted to be in such a vulnerable position. As a result, women would always leave him because he would not let them connect with him. This confirmed his story, "You can never count on women to be there." His story became a self-fulfill-

ing prophecy—the story created a reality guiding his actions which, in turn, reinforced the story.

Even though Drew's story led to increased frustration, at least it was for him a picture of reality that was familiar and known. It made him feel comfortable and secure. Simply being present to the unraveling of his story helped him settle down and examine his experience. He discovered that he did not have to hold on to the story to survive and that awareness did not destroy him. Drew gradually learned to trust me as a guide to the unknown and to fresh experiences of self and others. With this trust, he began to relinquish the old story, engage with women in new ways, and thereby construct a new life story.

The diagram in Figure 12 depicts the array of significant elements contained in Drew's and in all life stories as they are told in the "now."

Life stories are a composite of past, present and future as well as conscious and unconscious phenomena which affect clients' lives. The "now," as told in life stories, is a product of the past—as revealed unconsciously in dreams and in hidden conflicts, and consciously in memories, family myths and religious and cultural imprints; of the present—as experienced every day in relationships, actions and feelings; and of the future—as conveyed in expectations, aspirations and wishes.

GUIDELINES FOR DISCOVERING THE LIFE STORY

How can life stories become an integral part of the helping process? How can they be expanded upon? How can they be more than a static or sterile exercise? How can they be stereoscopic rather than sterotypic?

Unfolding life stories is a joint endeavor. To obtain meaningful history, be actively involved in a joint exploration with clients. There is no ready-made formula. Uncovering life stories cannot be reduced to rules. Do not follow a rigid or preconceived pattern to which the clients' narratives must conform. Be flexible. Offer clients latitude in selecting natural ways of telling their stories. Give

FIGURE 12. Dynamics of the Life Story

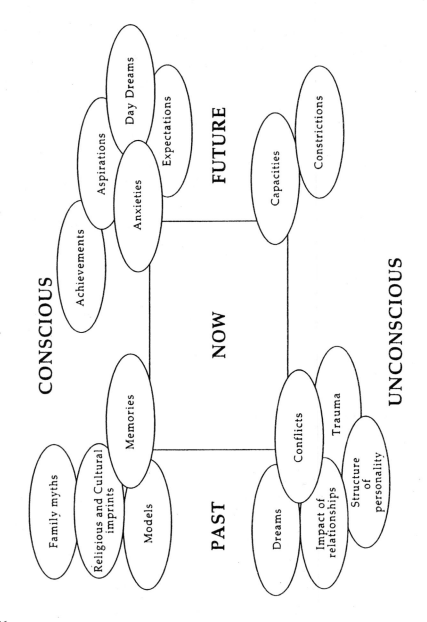

them general guidelines or suggestions. Explain what is relevant. Do not direct them, but rather invite them to tell you their stories in their own way. Such a common-sense approach is resourceful and humane. It also motivates clients to share their innermost selves.

Clients may respond quite easily and readily to your invitation. If they do not, do not be alarmed. There are other less threatening ways to elicit them. Some of these are discussed in other chapters.

These general guidelines may assist you in maximally encouraging clients to tell their story:

1. Be simple and succinct in giving direction: Overcomplicated instructions becloud the process.
2. Explain directly what information is desired.
3. Be alert to and enlist clients' unique style of storytelling and build upon it.
4. Proceed slowly and with care: neither rush nor force.
5. Strike a balance between when to lay back and when to prompt: it is only necessary to interrupt a spontaneous flow when clients are getting lost.
6. Give encouragement, being neither too gratifying nor too frustrating.
7. Help bring together the varied threads in an orderly manner. (Fox)

TWO CREATIVE METHODS FOR CAPTURING THE LIFE STORY

Two quite different but nevertheless effective methods of eliciting the life story are: the family tree or genogram and a personal inventory. Depending upon the clients' and your own style, these can be employed in unison or independently of one another to supplement your face-to-face verbal work with clients. They do not have to serve as adjuncts, but with uncommunicative clients can be the exclusive or principle vehicle for communicating. They are non-threatening methods for eliciting clients' perspectives on events, feelings, people, internal responses, dreams, day-to-day events, and much more. They have the advantage of allowing clients to unload emotional baggage. They are not a substitute for therapeutic

interaction but additional means to narrate the life story. Since human behavior is so complex, your efforts to change it require that
you draw upon as many sources of information and as many strategies as possible.

The Family Tree: Locating the Roots of the Life Story

Especially because of the interplay between family interaction
and family role and personality development, the utilization of the
genogram or family tree can maximize the effectiveness of individual and family intervention. Since clients' histories are constantly
evolving and growing, they are frequently elusive. The family tree
provides a diagram of a family over a few generations that grounds
repeating family likenesses and patterns (McGoldrick and Gerson).
It furnishes a clear picture of clients' nuclear families and the background of their formative experiences. The family tree continually
grows; it is not so absorbed with past roots that it neglects to notice
present modifications and branches. It creates an organic representation of relationships among family members—patterns of closeness, distance, conflict; it delineates boundaries, structures, and operating principles (McGoldrick and Gerson). It also gives access to
cultural, ethnic, socioeconomic and religious influences. Constructing a family tree together with the client, you can gain an understanding of the origin and development of the process of internalization and identification that determine projections enacted by the
client in current transactions.

Constructing the family tree together with clients is a felicitous
way of beginning work together because it neutralizes the tension of
self-exposure and the onus of self-blame. It reduces the stigma of
getting help. Emphasis is placed on the ecological context rather
than on the troubled individual. It reduces the sense of vulnerability
and permits deeper reflection on the interpersonal framework to
find out what is wrong so as to participate in the act of change. The
family tree can continue to grow throughout your work together. A
more expanded discussion of its relevance to family and individual
assessment and diagnosis appears in Chapter VIII.

The very process of scaling a family tree with clients is as meaningful as the information it conveys. The aim of the family tree is to formulate an overview of the dynamics and subtleties of role performance, interfamilial attachments and repetitive patterns. It is most illuminating, and perhaps even enjoyable, for both the client and yourself, especially when it follows clients' spontaneous musings, with you serving, at times, merely as a coach. You can be effective when simply following heuristic hunches — interjecting remarks, making comments, asking for clarification.

Although Chapter VIII elaborates on the use of the genogram in family assessment, the following brief example illustrates the usefulness of a family tree in helping to understand and to intervene to "un-stick" a troubled female client.

> Paula, a 27-year-old banking executive, sought help for her "sexual unresponsiveness." In an unconsummated marriage of four years, Paula and her husband, both ostensibly wanting children, were referred by their family physician for marital counseling. Paula's husband refused to participate in the process. Paula was distraught, self-blaming about her husband's unhappiness, but was unable to state this clearly and directly. She spoke haltingly only of a dissatisfying and dismaying sexual relationship. While she presented a clinical picture of vaginismus, most frequently treated by behavioral techniques, there was a deeper more remote and hidden underlayer to the phobia which required exploration; yet, Paula persistently resisted talking about her history, very likely because she felt it would manifest information she felt a need to suppress. I suggested our constructing a family tree. This seemed sufficiently neutral, even intriguing to Paula. She agreed and was motivated to proceed.

Figure 13 is an extended main branch of Paula's family tree yielding the repeated cycle of "broken" relationships. The genogram makes compelling what words only allude to — the unusual and uncharacteristic pattern of separations.

FIGURE 13

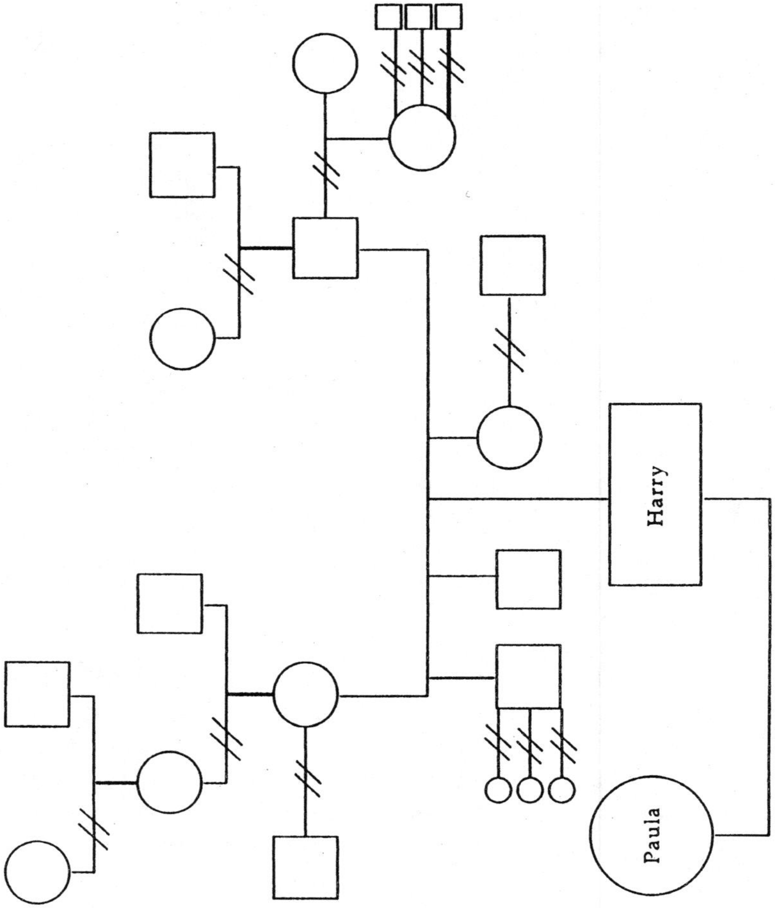

As we worked on and talked about her family tree together, it soon became apparent that Paula, the youngest of four siblings, was entwined in an intergenerational but disguised family ban on intimate relationships. Her two older brothers were each divorced twice; her stepsister was divorced three times and her natural sister was in the process of a divorce. Her mother and father had been married prior to their own union, and, in turn, both of them came from split families. This was extremely unusual for that earlier generation. In each situation, as she tearfully described it, there was a rancor and pervasive distrust in the relationships. The impermanence of relationships, a view of them as fragile and crumbling, led to recognition of her own conflict around attachments and abandonment; her ambivalence toward her father and, subsequently, her husband, repressed fear, anger and hostility and guilt about fantasized incestuous experiences. Recognizing that her sexual dysfunction was a means of symbolically expressing and sustaining a family pattern which she had internalized, she was able to make inroads on altering the self-defeating behavior that was being manifested sexually.

The family tree provided an important breakthrough for Paula and for me. It enabled both of us to get past the circumscribed presenting problem—vaginismus—which, if taken at face value would have been treated quite differently. Looking at a broader, more enriched picture of her family made possible a more accurate, inclusive and comprehensive assessment of the situation. At the same time it provided a means for deepened understanding and examination of the lineage associated with the problem. The mutual endeavor, understanding the life story, opened up channels of communication in the initial stage, improved assessment, decreased resistance and propelled us toward further work at resolution. Paula recognized that she saw her life through a filter of distortions.

The Life Inventory: Registering the Story

Another effective means of gathering data, especially in the initial phase of work, is to provide clients with a written inventory of questions and statements to guide them in recalling and then detailing their personal story. I use this method as a stimulus for ongoing reflection; it is not used merely as a "one shot" attempt to gather history. A series of comments or statements, some of which are amplified upon below, are intended to trigger clients' reflections about themselves and their situation and guide them in writing an autobiographical narrative.

Unlike standardized forms mandated in some agencies, which straight-jacket a *post dictum* account in a rigid fashion, this inventory is used flexibly. I suggest at the initial interview that the client take home the mimeographed inventory to peruse. The statements are instructions in themselves, insofar as they give clients an idea of the type of information I consider to be relevant to our ongoing work. It is, more significantly, a stimulant for them to recount reactions or responses in whatever way they wish. The writing helps to evoke memories, fantasies, and dreams, which, when not deliberately expressed, remain unrecognized. Putting thoughts and feelings into writing captures the ephemeral. It better promotes penetrating critical appraisal by the client and you.

There is no single set of statements that is uniformly or universally helpful either to clients or to clinicians. I developed the ones I use over time and continually revise them. You have your own theoretical orientation, method, style, and experience to guide your development of an inventory of statements or questions. It is important to remember that the inventory is intended to be suggestive, not absolute.

Just as there is no single set of statements that is uniformly helpful, there is no single way of responding to it. While some clients write out their responses discursively in notebooks of various sizes and designs, some clients choose other ways to express themselves. For example, one client wrote an "epic" about himself in rhymed couplets. Another client sang her responses. Some clients, wanting to answer more spontaneously than they felt writing allowed, spoke their responses directly into an audio recorder. This method makes it possible to hear their pauses, sighs, tears, laughter, etc., as they tell the story. It truly exposes much more of them.

Try not to let your own style interfere with the way clients naturally talk about themselves. When you are flexible, you not only facilitate the flow of vital information, but you give clients a rare opportunity to talk freely about themselves, and give yourself the opportunity to see them in action doing so.

I ask clients to pick and choose the order in which the statements are answered as it best suits their own situation and personality. Too, they are at liberty to find the method of responding that is for them the most comfortable and effective. Clients are encouraged to pose and answer their own questions as well. If you are required by agency policy or governmental regulation to use a particular stand-ardized format or questionnaire, employ it imaginatively. For ex-ample, hand clients one copy to examine while you fill out the second; allow clients to complete the form themselves at home; permit them to select the sequence and take responsibility for an-swering. There is nothing magical, mysterious, or secret about the need for historical data. In the long run, clients are the only ones who can provide accurate information anyway. When they are in-volved as fully as possible in sharing it, they are more apt to paint a full and clear picture.

Whether clients be individuals, couples or families, they are asked to complete the inventory. A remarkable result of its use by couples and families goes beyond the stimulus it provides for re-flecting on self. It provides a clearer view of clients' dynamic coun-terpoint.

My own inventory, revised over time, is comprised presently of 27 statements. A selected few appear below. Later in this chapter, three statements and the responses from three separate clients, including one couple, illustrate how the "telling" reflects clients' differing and unique styles of being and reacting. Five sample statements are:

7. Describe your feelings about your life during childhood, teens, and early adulthood.
21. Describe your present situation.
22. Describe the "significant others" in your life.
23. As you consider the whole experience of answering these statements, what insights, feelings or questions have em-erged?
26. Daydream! What are the most meaningful ways you see yourself living in the future? What are some of the things you

would like to accomplish for the future. Don't consider whether they are possible. Just daydream and record them.

These representative statements stimulate clients to muse about their past, present and future. They often come to appreciate the interconnection of all three time frames as they respond. Moreover, their account provides an avenue for your deeper exploration and examination.

Following are three statements with actual responses from three different clients. Their particular and different ways of responding demonstrate not only the rich and varied ways they perceive and define themselves and their experiences but also illustrate the value of the inventory in providing information and in sustaining the work.

The following minimal background is provided only to acquaint you with the three clients. I believe that you will find that their own statements paint an amazingly intimate, rich and accurate portrayal of them. Client A is a recreation counselor seeking assistance in coming to grips with two outstanding issues. He described the first as his "staying too long" in his present job where he kept "pouring himself out" without getting anything in return. He commented that his "staying too long" was a familiar pattern to him. He enunciated the second issue as "getting the guts" to marry a woman, fifteen years his junior, who had been a participant in a recreation group he led.

Clients B and C are unmarried partners. They came seeking couple counseling. They were gravely concerned about their increasing emotional estrangement following the birth of their son. They approached this transition in their lives so differently and found themselves unable even to converse with each other about it. They could not bridge the gap produced by their opposite styles of coping. Their responses to the inventory are particularly fascinating since the manner of their responses, combined with the content, sharply pinpoints the very conflicts and differences which caused them distress and brought them for help in the first place.

Incidentally, Client B's responses to the inventory occupied three typewritten pages; his partner C filled nine typewritten pages with her remarks.

Statement 1: Describe yourself.

Client A: I am a sensitive 31-year-old man. From 13 to 18 I was in the seminary and since that time I have devoted my life to working with young people. I have overworked to limit my personal life and now have a few close friends in whom I confide completely and many acquaintances but few people I socialize with regularly. I take criticisms to heart. I sometimes feel bad about myself even when criticism is wrong. I worry about things for which I am responsible so am therefore rarely remiss in my duties but I have great trouble relaxing. I am not outgoing and therefore do not socialize quickly. I take friendships and commitments very seriously; I am ambitious to the extent that I like to do a good job and be the boss, or at least be independent. But I become anxious in competitive situations.

Client B: 1. Describe yourself. 40. Aging hippie. Precise. Mind for detail. Continually trying to understand the world, unify conflicting ideas. Thoughtful and considerate. Strong willed.

Client C: The answer would vary considerably by the day. Today I'm tired but feel some accomplishment so there are mixed feelings about who I am. I am a woman of thirty-eight who appears younger. A new mother who works at home at two different jobs. I reach for different things with medium success. One friend described me as "caring so much and trying so damned hard." I would describe myself as worrying more than caring and as being too fearful to try enough.

Statement 13: Describe the atmosphere of the home where you grew up.

Client A: We did not have much money so we lived thriftily. My father worked hard, often at two jobs, to improve our economic situation. My parents were strict Catholics and they were about 20 when I was born. They were loving with me and saw that I was well disciplined. My mother's side of the family was Irish and they were less affectionate than my father's Italian/French culture. We spent much time together and although I was an only child for 7 years I was not spoiled because we lived simply. There was not any arguing or fighting or even friction between my parents.

Client B: 11. Describe the atmosphere of the home where you grew up. Many homes; many atmospheres. Until 19, lived with mother. Only child until 11. Pseudo father for younger brother. Both parents married twice. Mother divorced twice, father once. Up and down the socioeconomical ladder; ranging from upper to lower middle class. Apartments, near mansions.

Client C: From eight to thirteen our home was my mother and sister, both of which worked. Then ten of the twenty-three years at home, it was just my mother and I. The atmosphere was usually quiet as I was most often alone. But we always had animals and there was love and the three or two of us together. We spent a great deal of time sitting at the kitchen table but not usually eating. We all cooked for ourselves, which usually amounted to toast or TV Dinners. My mother instilled the belief that one could always work to make things better and that one always should. My big Christmas present when I was twelve was a sewing machine so I could make my own clothes which I did.

Statement 24: What are the major priorities, goals, dreams, and frustrations of your life right now? How would you see them changing over the next few years?

Client A: I am now concerned with changing from devoting my life to service to others at the expense of my own health to building a healthy personal life. My own happiness is a priority. I no longer want to be content with making others happy. I want to marry and have a family of my own. I want to stop taking on impossible tasks and do a good job with something manageable. Since I am in love with Peggy I want to marry her, help her get her career going if that is her wish, have a family if and when we see it being right for us, and devote my energies to us. Now I am spread too thin. I'm tired and burned out. I live too much through others. I am happiest when with Peggy.

Client B: No response recorded.

Client C: To make more of my life with B. Occupying myself with work and caring for my child. I've shelved those personal needs and desires. But they are what determine the quality of life. I very much want a happy home which to me is an enjoyable, loving environment with good society from within and without. I would like financial security and to insure I can provide the same for my children and family. The dream is tied with my frustration. It is a dream to produce a grand movie I am afraid I will not be strong enough to meet and foresee the all-encompassing producer's duties. I have to learn to deal fearlessly with the powerful personalities I am tied to. Too often I act like the little girl, the sweet darling looking to please her potentially wrathful parents. When I am through with the first picture I will know whether I want to continue that arduous career or go on to something else entirely. My work at _____ is just what I call bread and butter work. I would like to not need it anymore.

The life stories or autobiographies of clients based on this inventory have been invaluable in fathoming history, forming differential diagnoses and a relationship that served as the foundation of further exploration and change. Life stories offer penetrating glimpses into clients' lives and often unexpected insights that advance the helping process. Furthermore, at termination, they provide the clients' own "before" picture against which to assess the "after" picture upon the conclusion of clinical work.

Client A, imposed a time limit of three months on the helping process. The inventory made it possible for us to quickly specify and address current problems. Although his responses revealed long-standing dysfunctional patterns involving self-esteem, he chose not to work on them. In the case of couple B and C, lines of communication were opened between them as they shared their responses to the inventory in interviews with me. They used their responses as starting points to launch in-depth discussion of themselves, their backgrounds and their own relationship. Meeting over a period of approximately eighteen months, B and C's direct responses to the inventory told much about them, but, more interestingly, led to our traveling along informative and intriguing side paths. For example, taking these detours together helped bridge their treacherous emotional gap. B, who did not "talk," was able to revise his terse and sardonic fashion of interaction with C. He came to realize that his very manner, coupled by his offering pithy and practical "little lessons," served no purpose other than to make C feel rejected. Although being "rational" was for him the loving thing to do, it was not perceived that way by C. C learned to curtail her frustrated ramblings, which, in her attempt to "make contact" with B, ended up having the opposite effect. He would become more rational and distant from her. She, doing what she considered the loving thing, "reaching out," cut him off. He, reacting to her "unreasonableness," would become more impatient and closed. An impasse would typically occur, leading to total alienation, conflict and unhappiness. This destructive pattern of interaction was interrupted as they exchanged and discussed their responses to the inventory statements.

A critical component in enhancing their bond was the obtaining from the inventories an insider's view of each other's life "script." They came to recognize their own residual "stuff" from past experiences, triggered in the present situation. This led to dreadful re-experiencing of earlier pain, as if it truly existed in the present situation. Indeed, they saw how they fashioned this relationship to reproduce old scripts. Their roles changed after perceiving their parts in what they referred to as "this terrible circle." Reviewing the inventory facilitated interaction and the expression of affects, freeing them to hear and act on suggestions for experimenting with alternative modes of interrelating. Each also came to appreciate special assets and unique worldview of their partner.

For clients A, B and C, as for many others, the family tree and inventory have made it possible to capture and encapsulate the uniqueness of their language, skills, and perspectives. The "structure" of the inventory, paradoxically, frees them and you for spontaneous interaction.

REFERENCES

Fox, Raymond. "The Past Is Always Present: Creative Methods for Capturing the Life Story," *Clinical Social Work Journal*, 11 (4), 1983.

McGoldrick, Monica and Randy Gerson. *Genograms in Family Assessment*. NY: Norton, 1985.

Donald, Spence. *Narrative Truth and Historical Truth*. NY: Norton, 1982.

Chapter X

The Written Word: Enriching Your Work

The practice of psychotherapy should be interesting, appealing, and charming.

—Milton Erickson

Our subjectivity is our true home, our natural state, and our necessary place of refuge and renewal. It is the font of creativity, the stage for imagination, the drafting table for planning, and the ultimate heart of our fears and hopes, our sorrows and satisfactions. For too long we have dismissed the subjective as ephemeral and of little consequence; as a result we have lost our center and been magnetically drawn to the shallow harbors and arid beaches of unrelieved objectivity.

—James Bugental

Writing about oneself, others and events is a powerful resource for gaining perspective. Because of this, writing can be a valuable supplement to the helping process, stimulating self-observation and encouraging self-disclosure. This chapter demonstrates the multifaceted and flexible use of writing for you and clients and offers illustrative examples to demonstrate its efficacy.

CLIENT WRITING

Logging

Since restrictions of time limit either the depth or breadth of exploration in each face-to-face encounter with clients, writing in a log provides continuity to the work and can be used in a variety of ways. Entries can be assigned or free expression encouraged. Open-ended, directed, or semistructured, the log facilitates your having access to clients' memories, dreams, and everyday events. Clients' recorded reflections on content already discussed during sessions, or newly presented, amplify understanding for them and for you. Logging, therefore, continues the momentum of your work outside the formal structure of the interview, sustaining interest and focus in the helping process (Fox).

When a client brings you his or her log, draw from it in a nonconstrained and creative way. For example, you might read it at the beginning of your session as background, concentrate on it exclusively, or not refer to it at all. You might select portions of it to discuss further or put it aside to peruse at another time. However you use it depends upon the circumstances of your immediate exchange with the client. I introduce the idea of log-keeping in the initial interview, explaining its purpose and asking that in his or her first entry the client record impressions, questions, omissions, concerns, or whatever else comes to mind about our initial contact. This early use of the log familiarizes the client with log-keeping and provides valuable data in itself; more importantly, the way the client approaches log-keeping guides you in its differential use. If clients choose not to use the log, it is never forced, always discussed. The log provides an added perspective into clients' situations because, progressive and cumulative, it furnishes instant history and instant participation and allows both of you to examine progress at different stages of the helping process.

Finding Oneself Through a Scrapbook

The log can take many forms—concise outline, lengthy letter, essay, scattered phrases or words. The way clients express themselves offers a transparency of their life projected onto the page. For Peter, a 14-year old in foster care placement nearly all his life, the log, or "scrapbook" as he called it, became a declaration of his identity. Shifted between eight foster homes within 12 years, he was referred for help because of "poor memory," poor self-esteem, and presenting an elusive quality of being "lost." As we talked about his keeping a log, he proposed the idea of starting a "scrapbook" where he could organize the photographs and mementos that he secreted in many different places. In the course of our slowly, yet methodically, compiling a scrapbook together, Peter was able, as he gathered all the disparate pieces of his life into a unified whole, to piece together the fragments of his life. He was able, thereby, to clarify his memory of events and himself. As time progressed the "scrapbook" became a source book of his milestones. It included snapshots, baseball cards, ticket stubs, library cards, official documents, and other keepsakes, all with significant memory traces that he was able to recollect as they were glued in. Because they all helped set him apart and define who he was, the scrapbook enabled him to find himself, and to build a self-image. Peter was able to repair a fractured ego and establish an identity by working with me on creating his scrapbook and by expressing his thoughts and feelings.

Peter's log contained few words; Carol's log, on the other hand, was a word play.

Dialoguing: A Play for Self-Discovery

Carol, an aspiring actress, sought help for severe anxiety attacks, a sense of incompetence, and sexual unresponsiveness. She chose to unleash her thoughts and images in the log in the form of dramatic dialogue. The dialogue, as she wrote it, resembled a play script, which facilitated her expressing the conflict between her expansive needs and rigid conscience. She soon recognized that the dialogue represented polarities of her inner self. Fascinated by her own early discoveries, she played out these scripted roles. Eventually able to articulate and clarify her ambivalence and dichotomous modes of acting, Carol emerged with better understanding of her long-standing problems and sexual freezing. Finally, she discovered that these polarities were her inner scared child's attempt to fathom her mother's desertion and father's sexual abuse and at last could relinquish her self-blame and deprecation.

While it might be argued that some clients might misuse the log to avoid and rationalize, this has not been my experience. When it is employed with discretion, it leads to remarkably intensive self-analysis and honest disclosure (Fox).

This "structured" log was assigned to meet the unique character of the client and the demands of the therapeutic goal. An "unstructured" log can also achieve positive results as detailed below.

Open-Ended Discovery: Amplifying a Family Focus

An open-ended log often helps to loosen the constraints which have been built up for those whose fantasy life is minimal, who hesitate letting their imaginations run free, or who ignore inner irrational visions or intuition. "Stream of consciousness" entries enable these clients to gradually unfold and subsequently recognize and accept other than rational resources. Very often, paradoxically, for those with an excessive need for order and structure, and little tolerance for ambiguity, as well as for those who have difficulty in relaxing and contacting and observing a spontaneous flow of thoughts, feelings or images, the log provides impetus for less constrained expression during face-to-face interviews (Fox).

With one highly intellectual male, Jim, who denied and vigorously fought against the possible existence of any irrationality in his life, standard "talking" methods were employed during regular contacts to help him uncover suppressed and repressed feelings, but to no avail. It was only after Jim rambled in his log that he gained access to information and feelings of a more emotional nature. Logging reduced intellectualization and brought him closer to his experience.

> Initial entries were suggested to Jim. One of his first entries was to trace his family's genealogy, to locate and discover his roots. Stimulated by this essay, he discovered some important clues to his relationship with his father, a restringent, closed, and aloof immigrant. Writing freed Jim's associations and encouraged him to recall dreams and "log them in." (He first denied ever having dreams, and then claimed to have forgotten them.) He was, over time, able to remember dreams, first in fragments, then in their entirety. He recorded them in the log which helped him plumb an underlying and repressed concern

about the nature of his relationship with his father. This was explored in depth over many sessions as he continued to turn away from logical, sequentially ordered thinking, toward freer contact with experience and feeling.

Jim eventually recorded a dream of entering a tunnel where he met an older man half-way, a dream rather clearly connected with facing his father. In successively dealing with the unfolding dream, he surfaced inner conflicts laden with rage. Over time, the continual analysis of the appearance of his father in dreams, either literally or symbolically, allowed him to ventilate and explore his rage and its sources.

The log promoted our examining this powerful material which might otherwise have remained repressed, and certainly would not have surfaced as intensively in so short a time.

BENEFITS OF LOGGING

The log is particularly helpful for clients whose myopia, rigidity, over-control, or impoverished fantasy life preclude deep exploration of their own worlds, because of possible pain, shame, or failure. It allows clients to "walk through" situations, in either retrospect or prospect, tens of times, and loosens the grip of self-constriction. Clients who feel silly or foolish when facing new or unusual experiences recognize their delimiting patterns which have made them reluctant to enter relationships in the past. The log is helpful also to clients who do not acknowledge their own strengths, trust their own capacities, or appreciate their own skills. Just maintaining the log is ego enhancing; it offers a fresh start.

I have found the log to be especially successful with those clients who give up too easily or who do not start at all if they do not know the outcome in advance. Likewise, for those clients who cling to obsolete coping methods, the log stirs the imagination to novel ways, and to new possibilities — ones clients discover themselves (Fox).

Poetry: Connecting Past and Present

The log enables both you and clients to probe inner experiences, identify irrational patterns, and find connecting threads between the present and the past. Whatever clients perceive is based in some measure on their background, which the log invariably taps. While keeping a log is not strictly intended to locate historical sources, it does foster exploration. Entries provide valuable data about the multitude of ingenious strategies clients employ to camouflage troublesome feelings. The form of writing the client selects to express himself or herself speaks volumes as with Joan, a personnel executive, who sought help for depression after a broken marriage. The breakup rekindled "tapes from the past," as she phrased it, about her self-image. She felt impotent, worthless, and empty, and was particularly troubled by her interaction with men. She initially found it very difficult to verbalize her conflicts and pain to me, a man, but was sufficiently comfortable to unleash them in poetry. Verse allowed her to meter her feelings, but to do so in a disciplined way which kept rein on excessive or too rapid ventilation. At the same time, her poetry provided a poignant depiction of her internal life and hinted at sources of conflict. The following poem is excerpted from Joan's log:

> I wish I could say
> How hurt I am
> In pain but
> All I feel is the
> Gray, cold walls of canyons
> I have
> Walked too many times
> Before that even
> The plains of your face
> Are less familiar
> And the shadows of your eyes
> More strange
> I wish I could say I
> Miss you but today
> It seems the only

Touch I
Really
Know
Is granite
Nightmare fingers
Holding me fast
And hard so often
I could not breathe
But these have stayed
The hours with me
Touched my body when I slept
And now they are become
The hands of my lover
Much more than yours
I wish I could say I
Would even die for you but
I have died so many times for
So many things I did not know I
Cannot even count it seems
Even the ground would say
What you again

Joan's poem offers a penetrating picture of despair that led, in our face-to-face sessions, to discussing how the experiences in her youth had deadened her emotions and led so frequently to suicidal thoughts. We gained a clearer understanding of a core problem with her husband associated with that of her father. Initial inquiry elicited only a dispassionate statement about early sexual abuse by her father, who permitted, and witnessed, her repeated molestation by his friend. The poem unleashed long dormant and overwhelming feelings of rage, shame, guilt, and uncleanliness. It drew attention to negative attitudes toward herself and toward men and led us to trace the origins of these feelings back to repressed past experiences of abuse and rejection. I was able, furthermore, to encourage Joan's reaching her own interpretations about the relationship with me, promoting a corrective experience that deepened our alliance. Had our contact been restricted to verbal dialogue, and our conversation strictly focused on the presenting issues, it seems unlikely that it would have unfolded as successfully as it did.

Glimpses Back: Documents of Verisimilitude

The following example shows not only how the log was used by Elaine, a 30-year-old female client (whose background is discussed in Chapters VII and VIII), as an impetus toward deepened understanding, but how it motivated her to make available journals from adolescence, which, when examined, catapulted the work forward. Elaine's teenage journals provided a slice of time to examine and thereby an increased understanding of her particular dynamics. They pinpointed central problems, ideas, and fantasies.

In and out of therapy for over fifteen years, Elaine welcomed the opportunity to keep a log, having been discouraged by counselors to do so. An exceptionally bright youngster, she had started writing extensively during her preteen years in an effort to clear her mind. When she first entered a psychiatric hospital in her early teens, her therapists discouraged her from writing because they considered it a form of resistance. In her work with me, Elaine welcomed the log. She wrote about her history and background, and divulged, for the first time, her emotional reactions to past episodes in her life. She shared the entries with me but would talk no further about them. My responsiveness to her entries initiated her exploring them verbally. More significantly, she entrusted me with a series of unedited childhood diaries she had kept hidden since her lengthy treatment began in adolescence.

Elaine's teenage diaries were filled with thoughts, wishes, and dreams. They provided a rare and vivid picture of everyday events in her life as they occurred. They furnished a glance at her complex history and family dynamics. After thoroughly reading these diaries, I returned them to Elaine, asking her to reread them herself and to make marginal notes of her present associations to them. Our mutual study and discussion of the entries during sessions led us to focus on her relationships with men — her father, ministers, teachers and former therapists. The following entries concern her father:

12/26/62 — Daddy is downstairs throwing a tantrum because no one jumped to turn off the basement light the instant he told them to. Daphne woke up and started to cry. Did he care? No. If he would just be quiet, she would go back to sleep, but he has to keep yelling. If she does get up, he won't have to be the one to take care of her. Sometimes I can't stand him.

The following two more recent entries show Elaine's shift in attitude and feeling:

7/4/88 — I wish to exclude men from the human race. At first it was only as if they didn't even exist. Then they existed but in some way undefined, nonhuman — more beastlike; then as "people"; now finally as men and often as individual men.

11/6/89 — Spent last night with Harry. Interaction made me aware of how protective and defensive I am with men and I am, relatively speaking, far more open and relaxed with him. Particularly aware of this physically.

The value, of course, of having these earlier entries was inestimable. They offered a glimpse of how she perceived what was happening in her life as it happened, rather than in retrospect, with its additional distortions of recollection, editing, and selection. This is not to say that there were not distortions in perception at the time of the earlier writings. Distortions are present even as an event occurs, but there were not, to muddle reality further, the secondary distortions of the past as remembered. Parenthetically, of course, the choice of distortions themselves are a rich source to tap. Needless to say, the teen journals were a rich lode. Their exploration was a critical dimension in the entire helping process because they revealed how her present relationships with men were repetitions of her relationship with her father leading to still further analysis of her present interactions with men, including me. Focusing on understanding the development of maladaptive interpersonal relationships in the past, she untangled transferential reactions. As she discriminated between the past and the present, her present log, juxtaposed against earlier journals, enabled us to penetrate beneath the surface realities, documenting a shift from suspicion, fear, and bitterness toward men, to a greater degree of openness and trust.

Exposing her self without repercussions, she gradually exhibited new behavior outside sessions, in her transactions with men. This example illustrates how helpful logging can be in long-term work; it also has considerable merit in short-term treatment, as with Jose.

Logs in the Short-Term

Jose, a 32-year-old father of five, twice divorced and living with his lover, was hospitalized for a back injury he sustained from being beaten with a baseball bat by his present lover's husband. After his release from the hospital, his pain increased in his back, neck, shoulders, and head. His physician referred him because, after lengthy tests, there was no explanation for his experiencing so much pain, so frequently. In collaboration with his physician, I encouraged Jose to keep a sequential and detailed log of the time when his pain began and intensified and the circumstances involved prior to these feelings. He also recorded his reactions and way of coping. Keeping the log and reflecting on it with me enabled him to become aware that his emotional stress, connected to his being pulled in so many directions without respite, was directly related to the onset and maintenance of his pain and discomfort. Unwilling to explore this internal pressure, even though he noted it as relevant to his physical distress, he agreed only to an 8-week contract during which time he used the log, in conjunction with weekly visits, to master relaxation techniques and stress reduction exercises.

Angelic Intervention

Doodles, drawings, and sketches provide added sources of insight into the varied aspects of clients' personality and perceptions. Donna's log, for example, was a portfolio of angel drawings. At first, the angel's forbidding pose was like that found on cemetery pedestaled statues. Over the course of two years, the original pose softened; indeed, the angel descended from the pedestal and stood casually on the ground with a bemused smile on her face.

For Donna, raised with a rigidly religious background, the angel revealed her strict and punishing inner censor. She remembered having seen and continually dreamt of "fallen" angels and angels pursuing her for her misdeeds. Her drawings symbolically manifested her internal conflicts and tensions. These came more to light during interviews where she assumed these various angelic postures. She absorbed the experience and reflected minimally on it aloud in words, then slightly shifted her pose. Her drawings which traced changes in the angel's posture from a forbidding to a forgiving stance, reflected her own psychological metamorphosis.

GUIDELINES FOR USING A LOG

The following guidelines will enable you to maximize the log's effectiveness as a highly unique and individualized means for self-disclosure and development. Remain flexible and adaptable, remembering that the log

- is voluntary, not forced. Any pressure exerted to maintain it would discourage clients from fully and honestly expressing what is really going on in them.
- is not "graded" or "judged." It is not intended to be an ordeal, but, rather, an added opportunity to state ideas, beliefs, attitudes, feelings in whatever manner best suits the client's needs.
- works best when it is descriptive and explicit, expanding on themes in vivid detail, using concrete language, rather than generalities or abstractions.
- has a distinctive form that is as important as its content; its form is an integral component in the experience of expressing oneself.
- is intended to be spontaneous and honest: requirements and restrictions usually associated with writing are put aside, allowing freedom in self-expression. (Fox)

The absence of formal rules of structure, content, and style promotes ventilation, reflection, and description accelerating the growth process.

AN EXPANDED DIMENSION OF CLIENT WRITING

Noting Messages

Client writing can be of value in ways other than logging. For example, in some families and for some couples, verbal exchange inevitably deteriorates to name-calling and shouting matches. Indictments and rancor, rather than true dialogue, characterize the exchange. To prevent bouts of whining, arguing, or pleading, resulting from either a misuse or an overdose of talking, I suggest that such families and couples exchange notes to raise differences coolly and reasonably. Not strictly problem centered, note exchanging eases the awkwardness of expressing tender feelings or raw emotions, which, if not written, often remain unsaid. Notes offer family members a calmed and disciplined vehicle for giving each other encouragement, feedback, and advice as well as release of sentiments.

Letters of indignation, complaint or outrage are another purposeful use of writing. I encourage clients to write letters, even if they remain unmailed, to express aroused passions. Clients frequently suppress negative feelings and obsessively ruminate about what they "should have said." One client, for example, discharged his feelings of contempt in a letter to a public official who had supported legislation he found morally offensive. Reading and rereading it, he eventually sent it; more important than the relief he experienced from releasing his feelings was the satisfaction of a reply. An unexpected dividend was learning that uttering feelings rather than swallowing them can have impact and produce positive results.

Record Keeping and Agenda Making

I have found it useful in selected instances for clients to record interviews. This procedure may depart from one in which you exclusively document the work and keep notes. Have you heard clients say, "Gee, this session was good, I wish I had it to play back." I urge some clients to summarize their reflections in writing after sessions. Some clients literally take notes during the interview; still others actually audiotape it. Frank believed that he could not trust his memory to recall all the insights he gained during our interaction, so, in order to remember, he sat with a pen and pad poised on his lap, taking notes. Some clinicians would criticize this as resistance and claim that it would dilute the relationship. I have not found this to be the case. Over time, writing has become a productive adjunct to my work with clients. It gives us a chance to correct distorted beliefs and to review movement.

Another client, Mike, prepares agenda for sessions. In order to recall what had happened to him between visits, he formulated an agenda for each session which in itself had a cathartic effect and enabled him to sift through concerns and generate ideas to face them. In handing me an agenda, he felt secure that "at least superficially, all bases are covered." When Mike could not address all the items on the agenda, he felt secure in knowing that he had in advance given me a "bird's eye view" of his previous week. We could focus on one item, or put aside the whole agenda to attend to more immediate concerns which he, having "filled me in," was freer to examine.

Agenda setting is especially helpful for clients who ascribe equal importance to all events. It permits them to realign thinking, set priorities, and decisions. This was the case with John, a seriously depressed 22-year-old postal employee with a severe learning disorder that prevented him from completing high school. His weekly agenda written on index cards relieved his frustration of not being able to "share all," and freed him for more deeply feeling his loss, pain, and grief during sessions. A sample of his agenda over a six week period, exactly as written, follows:

11/8—(1) want to know again if its' O.K. for me to feel like your a step parent to me. (2) I don't like how my family develop thru the years, and wish it was better (3) party for Laurie (4) Monday: how I felt growing up, very hard to show how painful my life is every day (5) This week: Feeling not good enough, have nothing feel so alone, what other have—I don't have having friends, developing a relationship with a girl Being liked by other people; and for me I need to feel it so bad, I **really feel bad, I feel like crying**

11/28—(1) show concern for me, about being late and how it made me feel. (2) feeling SAD about no friends (3) some days I wake up feeling depressed, I stay like that for hours (SUNDAY) (4) I've been feeling, lonely, SAD, angry, dejected, a sense of hopelessness, bitter about the way I develop, feeling very fragile when I'm in certain situations or certain songs, wanting things to be better (5) Feeling sorry for my parents awful marriage, but at the same time feeling VERY ANGRY at them for the mistakes they made. Also, wishing my parents could have been more like some one else's parents (6) Having too many unhappy feelings and not enough happy ones XXXXXXXXXX Having XXXXXX so many feelings towards you, and for me to be allowed to express them verbally and in writing to you, means so much to me.

12/2 – (1) When I left your office on Monday, I felt confused and I feel I don't have the ability to understand every thing you try to explain to me. (2) Monday and Tuesday were very trying and sad days for me. Monday: it was hard to be at work Tuesday: late at night, I put on that album and I became very sad. What I feel about a song is probably very different than what the song might mean, if it has one. Also, had another dream, where you were the main person in it. (3) In general, just feeling very sad about everything. It's so hard for me to go on with life, when I have no friends and almost nothing else but work. I don't feel good about myself. I just feel so lost and depressed about life in general and the way things are going, it hurts so bad.

John's agendas gave me penetrating revelations that he could not talk about. The agenda made it possible for him to develop increased clarity about himself, his family, me, his life and the helping process. The writing helped him to locate underlying sources of his depression, to touch affects, and gradually open discussion and channel it toward avenues of relief and redirection. Our contacts increased as a result of the agenda. He began slowly to experience relief from his torment as it was openly released, increased energy which he directed into structured social activities, and a more positive outlook on himself and his life.

The very act of preparing agenda fosters orderly and discriminating thinking. It stimulates clients' acuity in focusing attention on specific issues.

Critical Incidents

One additional useful method of client writing is critical incident reporting. Here the client identifies a specific "charged" event with as much specificity as possible. The description includes relevant details and circumstances surrounding the event, people, and the role that the client plays. This is followed by brief summary and analysis. The helping interview, for example, may itself be precisely one of these events. Musings in writing capture crucial episodes, patterns of response, and the interdependence between the helping process and real life. They are a core mechanism of communication, and their review helps direct focus. Reports of these critical incidents become reliable means for monitoring thoughts, actions, and feelings when they are fresh in clients' minds. They are a running account of the chronology of the changes that occur during the helping process. These narratives are not stuffy or static descriptions but dynamic unfoldings which reveal how clients draw upon their understanding to make meaningful connections, decisions, and problem solve.

YOUR OWN WRITING

Writing About Yourself

Writing need not be restricted to clients. There are various ways that writing can be a valuable tool for you as well. Writing your own log, for example, has all the same benefits for you that it has for clients.

Writing about your own life experience is one of the best ways to give new meaning to your present personal and professional life. It also enables you to make an appropriate separation between the two. Certainly it is an excellent way to understand your own past more fully. Writing your own autobiography puts your own contradiction, paradoxes, ambivalances and unfinished business into perspective. Fathoming your own personal identity can be instrumental in freeing you from superimposing yourself, in unhelpful ways, into clients' lives. Consider composing a metaphoric life story. For example, imagine your life as a river and describe how it flowed from its source, how it branched off, where it was damned up and how it got to where it is. Think of yourself as a playwright preparing a script. Create and review scenes, the roles you played in them to convey the dramatic tension in your life. Your writing, as with clients', clarifies your situation and better defines you. The very act of writing is a new venture and a new behavior breaking ground. I have found "clustering" to be a particularly valuable method for self-discovery.

Clustering

Clustering is a method of open-ended writing, akin to free association, developed by Gabriele Rico. It gives shape to your experience. It is a writing approach that forms and structures the confusion that sometimes characterizes our inner and outer world, especially when we are faced with a dilemma, impasse, or vague ache. Beginning with a nucleus word and spilling off other words and phrases at random, complex images and emotional qualities associated with them become clear, leading to a pattern and organization of meaning not originally perceived.

To start, on a blank page, circle a chosen stimulus word or phrase that comes to mind. Let your mind flow and write down other words that you associate to it, each in its own circle which radiates from the first. Connect the circles with lines. Start again when you have a new or different association. If it does not flow in any particular order, let each association find its own place. Be receptive to what comes. Don't censure. When you have exhausted this "playful" association, suspend your circling. Begin to write. You will be amazed at what comes together, at how the most troublesome thoughts can turn out to have unexpected depth and resonance. Figure 14 is a schemata of what a typical cluster might look like.

Starting from the word "transference" the cluster expanded into five directions each with very different types of associations, until the sixth direction led to "blank," ending the process. The translation of the cluster into a definition of transference led to this statement: "Transference is psychoanalytic jargon for a Freudian con-

FIGURE 14. Clustering

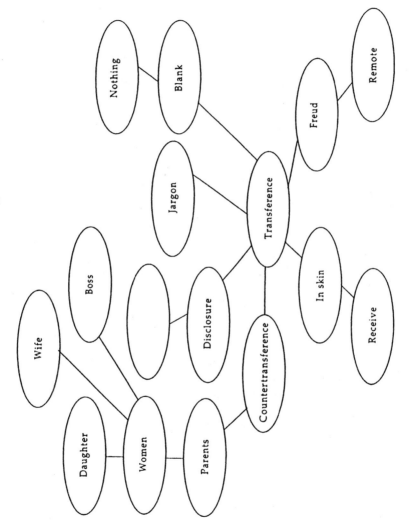

cept, developed in the remote past, explaining a client's uncanny, 'under the skin,' response to a person in the present, duplicating one from the past that rightfully belongs to his or her parents: for example, Larry inappropriately feeling rejected by his wife, boss or daughter whenever they are involved with other people because as a child he felt 'left out' by his mother whenever she was engaged in activity that did not include him, for example, playing bridge with friends. This phenomenon, once disclosed, leads to insight and changed behavior. Countertransference is the helper's transference.''

Clustering is a kind of brainstorming process beautifully explained by Rico. It is a process of creative writing that can be freeing for you as well as for clients. It helps you to contact inner process and gain self-awareness by accessing memories, freeing emotions, and capturing forgotten experiences. I highly recommend it to you as I do to clients.

Writing to Clients

Writing to clients can sustain and improve communication. Verbal interpretations to clients, for example, can be easily distorted, ignored or repressed. Written messages which reinforce these oral interpretations are tangible, visible, and hard to repress. The same is true of advice and prescriptions.

Writing is notably helpful in couple and family work where there is considerable potential for distortion. Writing to families and couples has many advantages, including:

1. clarifying your perceptions and observations
2. breaking impasses or repetitive destructive patterns
3. expanding and accelerating the work
4. confronting issues that are denied and avoided
5. specifying vague issues
6. desensitizing emotionally charged issues.

I ask families and couples to post a copy of my correspondence on their refrigerator so that it is visually present as a reminder to them whenever they go for a bite to eat. This may identify certain tasks they are to perform, remind them of homework they agreed to do, or post time schedules for specified interactions. Messages to clients should be short, no more than a page long. They should consist of no more than two or three main points. When they are longer, they become burdensome for clients, they are harder to digest. The ultimate effect can be to overwhelm rather than clarify.

ABOUT WRITING

In all its forms, writing is an efficient and effective tool for observation and disclosure. It is not a substitute for, rather an enhancement to, interactive person-to-person transactions. It helps clients and you to capture ideas, feelings and behavior in unique ways. It is a powerful tool for developing a high level of awareness. It facilitates communication. It can provide a bridge in relationships and can supply information that might otherwise be too overwhelming or too painful to face in verbal discussion.

Writing puts clients and you in touch with patterns of behavior, feelings and thinking and adds coherence to memories, fantasies, thoughts and intuitions. Its impact on both of you is great, and invariably leads to deeper understanding. Writing enriches the helping process.

Advantages of Writing

You may wonder, with all the paper work you already have, how you will find the time or inclination to deal with the various forms of writing I have suggested since they can seem so time-consuming and burdensome. Very likely the long records you keep are neither relevant nor helpful in your ongoing interactions with clients; however, the advantages of writing are more than fringe benefits. Writing helps clients and you in profound ways. It enables both of you to gain clearer access to rich interdependent complexities and multifarious dimensions that make for success in the helping process. Some advantages of writing bear repetition, and others should be more clearly explicated:

1. Writing encourages a stance of inward attention.
2. It develops a degree of comfort in self-observation and self-reporting.
3. It heightens self-awareness and fosters alternative ways of viewing oneself.
4. It establishes a sense of competence in being able to discipline and reveal oneself, which is ego-enhancing.
5. It lends itself to incisive self-reflection, especially when entries are reviewed over time.
6. Writing supports an appreciation of strengths, rather than debilities, in patterns of thinking, feeling, and behavior.
7. It helps trace the antecedents and consequences of patterns of thinking, feeling, and behaving.
8. It unfreezes thinking and feeling, making possible reinforcement of movement and change.
9. It heightens sensitivity to others and their conduct in relationships.
10. It documents clients' progress while going through the helping process.
11. Writing helps clients and you to be more receptive to spontaneous perceptions.
12. It helps you better attune to what is happening within clients.
13. It provides you with comprehensive data about clients.
14. It provides, for both clients and you, continuity during breaks and other separations.

An important dimension of writing is that it can provide a "before-after" picture of the helping process. Particularly at the time of termination, although at any interval along the way, it provides tangible documentation of change.

REFERENCES

Fox, Raymond. "The Personal Log: Enriching Clinical Practice," *Clinical Social Work Journal*, 10 (2), 1982.

Rico, Gabriele Lusser. *Writing the Natural Way*. Los Angeles: J. P. Tarcher, Inc., 1983.

Chapter XI

The Termination Process

Human beings are not victims of traumata from birth to death; they can find fulfillment in experiences that are hard to leave.

—Jesse Taft

What we call the beginning is often the end. And to make an end is to make a beginning. The end is where we start from.

— T.S. Eliot

Any ending is tough. Ending a helping relationship is especially so. Perhaps that is why we rarely hear people say "good-bye." Instead we hear such expressions as, "Be good," "Take care," "See you later." The very expression, "Good-bye," originally meaning, "God be with ye," has been abbreviated to "bye," perhaps to soften the pain of dealing with leaving and separation. As one client explained about termination:

> it means splitting, leaving, going away forever. It's feeling lousy, like crying, like relief from a burden, responsibility; it's all the things you did, and all you didn't do—right, wrong, everything but indifference, because you really cared about them. That's why it's so painful. That's why it's so damned hard to express.

"Good-bye," is avoided as if it is a curse because the words arouse acute and threatening feelings of loss, permanent separation, and foreshadowings of death. If "good-bye" is not uttered, the ending it signals does not have to be faced; yet, only when you and the client say "good-bye" to each other will you and your clients know the success of your work. I frequently share with clients a quip I heard long ago: successful helping is like successful parenting—it is self-obliterating.

Terminating the helping relationship concludes a unique interpersonal endeavor and signals a transitional process for you and your clients. In either case, it arouses pain; however, it can be, at the same time, a powerful and significant experience of growth, a marker of change. When skillfully handled, termination has the potential to put to rest failures at past endings.

NECESSARY LOSSES

Termination is not a unique occurrence in daily life or in professional functioning. To be alive is to be faced with continual separations, seldom dealt with squarely. It is no wonder, then, that terminating such an intimate association as the helping relationship evokes sadness and triggers unfinished business from previous losses and separations invariably experienced in the cycle of life from birth to death (expected—birth, first day at school, graduation, and abrupt—death, abandonment, divorce).

Judith Viorst catalogues these losses so well:

> Somewhat wrinkled, highly vulnerable and non-negotiably mortal, I have been examining these losses. These lifelong losses. These necessary losses. These losses we confront when we are confronted by the inescapable fact . . .
>   that our mother is going to leave us, and we will leave her;
>   that our mother's love can never be ours alone;
>   that what hurts us cannot always be kissed and made better;
>   that we are essentially out here on our own;
>   that we will have to accept—in other people and ourselves—the mingling of love with hate, of the good with the bad;
>   that no matter how wise and beautiful and charming a girl may be, she still cannot grow up to marry her dad;
>   that our options are constricted by anatomy and guilt;
>   that there are flaws in every human connection;

that our status on this planet is implacably impermanent;

and that we are utterly powerless to offer ourselves or those we love protection — protection from danger and pain, from the inroads of time, from the coming of age, from the coming of death; protection from our necessary losses.

These losses are a part of life — universal, unavoidable, inexorable. And these losses are necessary because we grow by losing and leaving and letting go. (Viorst, 2-3)

How clients and you approach termination reflects how we have dealt, probably miserably, with farewells in our lives up to this point. But this can change. You need not muddle through. Termination upsets and threatens the steadiness of your relationship; it also challenges you to discover more satisfying ways to separate. Loss, alarm, rejection, and helplessness are feelings that often overcome us when relationships end. You, however, the helper, are obliged to acknowledge, accept, and discipline your feelings so that you can speak the unspeakable "good-bye." You may know this, intellectually, yet are often so concerned with helping clients work out their feelings that you ignore your own. In not confronting your own feelings, you ultimately cheat clients of a full and shared experience. Actively address clients' central issues and feelings about termination; but first, candidly face your own.

It is easy to "overlook," "forget," or "bypass" all the painful feelings that termination arouses, but when you do, you disrupt the process and disturb clients. Do not preoccupy yourself with looking for a ready-made formula for a "smooth ending"; none exists. And, furthermore, the looking distracts you from fully experiencing *this* ending.

This chapter explains how termination can, at the same time, bring closure to your present relationship with the client and offer him or her an opportunity to resolve older ones. Depending upon how you approach it, termination can be a dismal undertaking or a catalyst for growth. While termination determines the degree to which therapeutic gains are maintained, when termination is a stimulating experience, it can bring clients and you to increased levels of integration and maturation.

LEVELS OF TERMINATION

Termination is the culminating stage, an end point in a total therapeutic process. It is also a discrete entity having its own distinctive stages with specific characteristics.

Termination: An End Point

Endings have their roots in beginnings. An integral part of a larger multifaceted process, termination gives you both an opportunity to review and tie together, retrospectively, the entire helping endeavor. Reiterating and scrutinizing the results of what you set out to accomplish reinforces and stabilizes change.

A microcosm of the entire helping process, your impending departure, as your initial presence, heightens clients' anxiety. The client reexperiences a separation/individuation crisis manifested by an ambivalent pull between his or her desire for independence and wish for dependence (Webb). Termination provides more than an opportunity to reinforce gains; it offers still another chance to recognize and modify conflicts. One reason why termination is frequently so unsatisfying is your failure to differentiate between task accomplishment and relationship ending. Often, clients who report improvement in their functioning and accomplishment of contracted goals are reluctant to leave. It is the relationship with you that they want to preserve.

Clients experience the beginning of the helping process as an ending. You helped them to stop clutching at untenable patterns and assisted them to reach toward untested ones. In ending the helping process, clients confront yet another beginning, but alone, because they leave behind your support which accelerates their fear of losing what has been gained and of facing an uncertain future. From this fear grows anxiety of separation echoing anxiety felt in the beginning. Impending termination revives old feelings and stirs up new ones. All need to be ventilated and resolved.

Termination: A Distinctive Process

Termination stands apart from other phases of the helping process having its own phenomenology and dynamics that resemble crisis intervention. The "precipitant" event is any announcement of impending termination which shifts the focus of your work from resolution of clients' problems, as such, to exploration of anxiety, and the defenses against it, connected with separation. Even though clients often consider it as a "little death," termination can enliven and intensify your relationship. Wanting to hold on to the familiar and comfortable, clients' motivation is renewed to accomplish much in a little time. Take advantage of this release of energy and channel it toward dealing with the reality of ending.

Consider these remarks by Harry, a thirty-four-year-old social studies teacher, when termination was at hand:

> This is a powerful place. There has been a lot of hard work and struggle. With results. It's hard to leave the center of some of your greatest triumphs. I'd like to stay. I know I have to go.
>
> You have been very important in my life and instrumental in my growth. It will be hard not to see someone you care about and trust — even my family and best friends don't know what you know.
>
> I often left your office upset, but never hopeless.
>
> Let's pull things together. I think I'm ready, no, I'm sure I'm ready.

Webb suggests that during ending, as in crisis, clients simultaneously feel happiness, exhilaration, anxiety, and loss about the prospect of being on their own. Many of the principles of working with clients in crisis, therefore, apply to termination. Webb outlines these relevant crisis principles in Figure 15.

TASKS IN TERMINATION

To assist clients to make a successful transition from being clients to being on their own, the eight tasks listed below should be carefully integrated into the process of preparing to separate:

1. Determining when to start termination
2. Evaluating progress and goal accomplishment
3. Working out conflict between acknowledging improvement and separating from help
4. Acknowledging and mourning the loss of the relationship
5. Recognizing and working through ambivalence
6. Discussing how progress can be transferred to other issues client may encounter in the future
7. Planning how to maintain gains and continue growth
8. Letting go.

SIGNS OF CLIENTS' READINESS FOR TERMINATION

What are the signs of clients' readiness for termination? In general terms, these include clients discovering their own potential, experiencing increased feelings of mastery, demonstrating an ability to take charge of their own lives, all of which become integrated functions in their day-to-day living. Ten specific checkpoints for assessing individuals' and ten more for assessing families' readiness for termination are listed below:

Individual Checkpoints

1. Approximate freedom from initial problems
2. Relief from anxiety and unrealistic expectations
3. Improved adjustment and coping with reality
4. Increased awareness, appreciation, and acceptance of self
5. Willingness to assume responsibility for own actions
6. Decreased complaining about the unfairness of life
7. Reduced dependency
8. Expansion of personality to include previously disowned characteristics
9. Enhanced sense of humor; laughing at self
10. Recognizing that life is not simple, predictable, or controllable.

Family Checkpoints

1. Family members seeing each other as distinct individuals
2. Tolerating, perhaps enjoying, differences
3. Loosening bonds
4. Resolving problems at home
5. Communicating directly and clearly
6. Developing outside relationships
7. Expressing strong positive and negative feelings
8. Risking new behaviors
9. Differentiating individuals from the family mass
10. Repairing emotional ruptures.

SEPARATION PARADOX

Termination arouses dread and anxiety and a desire to escape the stimulation causing it; simultaneously, it triggers an impulse to turn for relief to an "attached figure," to soften the blow. Ironically, in the complex interplay between clients and you, each of you is, for the other, the figure both of separation and of attachment. In this instance, you are the source of both unpleasant feelings and of comfort. Because they have depended on you for relief from suffering, when clients face losing you, they will grieve. Their grief will be accompanied by a mixture of other feelings — anger, alienation, and confusion, which will be defended against and manifested only indirectly.

Clients, during termination, may feel paradoxically closer to you for "sticking by" them during leave taking, while experiencing a sense of growing estrangement. This "close" yet more "distant" feeling, this dilemma of ambivalence frequently stirs in them a natural urge to preserve the familiar and ignore the inevitable ending. While clients might be terrified by deeper feelings and pull back from them, you need to be ready and willing to plumb them since you have the responsibility to interrupt such avoidance. Deal directly with your own feelings and actions as well; otherwise, you might unwittingly collude with clients' denial, evasion, or flight.

FIGURE 15

CRISIS PRINCIPLE	APPLICATION TO TERMINATION
1. Appreciate the crisis time-frame (6-8 weeks)	1. Allow adequate time to work through the crisis of termination.
2. Analyze the underlying meaning of the crisis for the individuals involved	2. Identify elements of *loss*, *threat*, and *challenge* which the termination precipitates for both client and worker
3. Deal with the *Loss*; Promote and facilitate the grief process	3. Discuss feelings associated with the loss of the therapeutic relationship (anger, deprivation)
4. Deal with the *Threat*; Recognize and interpret anxiety which underlies symptom formation	4. Review original reason for seeking help; identify progress; confront impulse to regress
5. Deal with the *Challenge*; Convey belief that a crisis is an opportunity to learn new coping	5. Analyze anxiety vis. à vis. separation/individuation issues (feelings about independence and autonomy)
6. Encourage cognitive awareness of significance of feelings	6. Verbalize the ambivalent, fluctuating feelings
7. Focus on the present	7. Work on the termination of the helping relationship
8. Offer anticipatory guidance	8. Help client rehearse future actions
9. Communicate therapeutic optimism	9. Let the client leave with belief in future independent survival

(Webb, 1985, 338)

Self-Awareness

You may feel a genuine sense of loss as work with clients ends, especially if it has been gratifying and productive. Acknowledging and bringing to rein your own feelings about separation will free you to be more attentive to clients' feelings. The success of termination, indeed, the success of the entire helping endeavor depends on your sensitivity to your own feelings. Among these feelings are sorrow, delight, wish for gratitude, all of which, if unexamined, depress the exchange with clients. Taking stock of your feelings reduces the chance of interfering with clients' expression of their own.

The outcome of termination — relieving clients' fears of abandonment and helping them accept separation — depends upon such factors in clients and in you as the quality of your particular relationship, the perceived degree of success or satisfaction within it, the degree to which earlier losses of significant persons have been faced, and the level at which mastery of the separation/individuation crisis has been achieved. You will improve the chances for a successful termination when you

- remain sensitive, flexible, empathic, and observant
- non-critically respond to clients' needs for security
- communicate continually in an open and direct fashion
- interrupt barriers inhibiting expression of feeling
- offer honest expressions and explanations
- state thoughts briefly and simply
- answer questions
- use concrete and familiar examples.

STAGES IN TERMINATION

Termination for clients is a multiple conclusion. It marks the end of this interpersonal relationship with you as a real person, a transferred object, and a helper. While clients react differently to this multi-dimensional ending, some being compliant, some oppositional, certain reactions commonly occur in progressive and predictable stages. Alert to the onset and progression of these stages you are better able to assist clients to express feelings accompanying them which might be ordinarily withheld or repressed. You are also better able to distinguish and help them distinguish between feelings that are induced specifically by this ending and those that are residual, that is, originating from past relationships but reawakened and projected onto this relationship. Understanding this distinction allows you to address both.

Perspectives on Stages of Termination

Kübler-Ross identifies five progressive stages for dealing with loss — denial and isolation, anger, bargaining, depression, and acceptance. These pertain, as well, to loss sustained during the ending phase of the helping process. In the first stage, denial and isolation are erected as defenses against the reality of separation. Clients, not accepting the approaching ending, make little attempt to deal with its reality, often acting as if you never mentioned it. In the second stage, anger, clients express hostility and lash out at you or others close to them. The ending of any meaningful relationship causes distress; things will never be the same. Familiar and comfortable in their relationship with you, clients, naturally, want to hold onto it; anything that hints at its dissolution, provokes anger. In the third stage, clients might bargain with you to maintain the relationship even at the cost of therapeutic gain. They try "to make a deal" to forestall the inevitable ending. Another client strategy is presenting an 11th hour problem or crisis. A common client strategy during this stage is negotiating a change in the relationship or modifying the contract, subtly conveying that they will be irked by your refusal to agree to new terms. Depression, the fourth stage, sees clients obsessing about the loss rather than working it through. The fifth stage, acceptance of separation, entails putting to rest the feelings attendant to all stages in order to avoid depositing old feelings into new relationships.

Another approach to loss and managing its effects is offered by Fox et al. captured in the following chart:

Major Affect	*Management of Affect*
1. Sadness or grief over loss	Initial denial or other defense against impending loss
2. Anger at the worker for leaving or at self for not being able to be left	Period of emotional reaction and expression of sadness, hurt, anger
3. Narcissistic wounds based in disappointed expectations	Working through of these feelings

Different in some respects from Kübler-Ross' approach, both frameworks underscore common themes — an initial period of denial, a period of hurt and anger, and a thrust toward resolution and acceptance. A further theme pervades the termination process but is not explicated by these writers — the constant struggle toward maturity and independence propelling clients toward health. While stages infrequently proceed according to the neat sequence suggested by these outlines, knowing their character attunes you more fully to clients' underlying dynamics.

How clients uniquely advance through the stages of ending and how they manifest affects is related to the nature of their problem, the state of their ego, the quality of their relationship with you, their emotional involvement in the helping process, and how well their earlier separation experiences were handled. Your sensitivity and timing will make it possible for them to ventilate feelings at successive phases and to move on to the next. When feelings are not talked out, they are acted-out in defeating ways.

TERMINATION TROUBLES

Tuning into You

At termination clients are exquisitely attuned to your feelings and how forthrightly you handle, project, or act them out. They may capitalize, consciously or unconsciously on this awareness to provoke or manipulate you to continue the work. Their motive is simple — to distract both of you from the real pain of separation and to hide feelings associated with it. In provoking you to behave in certain ways, they can justifiably react. These maneuvers are ingenious but they sidetrack you from the issue at hand, permit clients to conceal their true emotions and thoughts, or evoke guilt in you or in clients. Remember, clients' acting-out requires your complicity.

Unaware of your own feelings, you are less aware of the clients' and are therefore more susceptible to manipulation. Your vulnerability is increased further when you are stressed or have conflicts of your own related to separation. You may feel, for example, that by terminating you are deserting or betraying clients whose only relationship of trust is with you. As a result, in an attempt to assuage your guilt, you may minimize your importance or that of the helping process — acting distant or, the reverse, overprotective. Intercepting this message, and alert to its underlying meaning, clients may behave in ways to cause you even more guilt. On the other hand, they may act in ways to convince you that your leaving reflects a lack of caring or results from their "bad behavior." Clients may even act-out somatically, once again drawing you closer. A vicious interactive cycle is maintained by all the interactions mentioned above that effectively defeats your appropriately dealing with the real issues of separation.

Clients do not necessarily set out to dupe you; rather, their response is usually motivated by a desire to hold on. They may idealize or patronize you. Some other clients, possibly keyed into your needs for gratification, may attempt to convince you that whatever changes they made, they made expressly for you and tacitly threaten to resume maladaptive behavior unless you continue to work with them. Making it up to them to feel better yourself, offering excessive reassurance and advice and "catching" their symptoms, risks their sensing your inappropriateness and, indeed, reverting to former patterns of behavior.

The prospect of ending the helping relationship raises clients' insecurities about being on their own. If you ignore the real issue of separation, you cheat clients; feelings go unaddressed and unrelieved. Clients therefore understandably question the validity or value of whatever work you have accomplished. When you "play avoidance games" with clients, you precipitate regression. A premature and sometimes abrupt rupture in the relationship may ensue, precipitating negative feelings in clients and in you.

Sometimes clients feel intimidated or helpless and act like obedient children telling you only what you want to hear and refraining from criticism or hostility. Other times, feeling out of control or frustrated, they may blurt out anger and resentment. Accept and examine all these reactions; not doing so confirms their dread that no one has control and complicates the working-through process by justifying their sense of futility. Your own fear of clients' hostility or your own need to be liked may lead you to ally yourself with their anger. If you do so, both you and your clients will feel victimized.

When you are unable to manage your own feelings you may blame clients for causing you pain and you may then respond inappropriately: in direct ways — with abuse, criticism, or hostility, or in indirect ways — with displeasure or subtle discontent. A sense of rejection results which they translate, to protect themselves, into ways to reject you, often by leaving prematurely, in effect saying, "You can't fire me; I quit."

You may feel unsuccessful, not having rescued clients from distress. You may blame and persecute them for not having met your expectations and needs, thereby, eliciting anger from clients and becoming the victim of their legitimate feelings. When not assuming responsibility for your own feelings and actions, you contribute to clients' feelings of unworthiness, helplessness, and powerlessness, all with damaging results. Catching clients' feelings, pulling away, denying or displacing your own feelings, and detaching yourself from the experience of separation, leaves clients feeling abandoned, which, undermines the entire helping process.

THREE PHASES OF TERMINATION

Avoiding Pitfalls

Devote sufficient time to termination. Whether termination is suggested by clients or by you, it should not be abrupt, but should be introduced well in advance of the actual date of departure to allow sufficient time to discuss all the facets involved — cognitive, affective and behavioral. It is always important to give notice and reiterate, from time to time, the impending ending; importance grows in direct correspondence to the length and intensity of your relationship. Clients deserve the opportunity to enter, understand, and work-through, productively and systematically, each successive stage of disentanglement from the helping process and from you. Clients fear leave-taking and react to their lack of control over its happening. You can help them to discover strength in overcoming their painful reactions to parting. Draw upon their adaptive capacity to help them understand and deal with separation; they will not merely survive it but experience it as growth-producing.

Tying Up Loose Ends

Prepare for termination by examining what you believe has been accomplished in your work together. Review progress objectively and in detail, taking account of what goals have and have not been achieved. Consult your original contract and read your case record for evidence of change. Acknowledge the specific ways in which clients have promoted their own progress; credit yourself for your own contributions. Recognize and name other factors which have positively and negatively influenced the change effort — maturation, environment, friends, etc.

Prepare clients for the ending of the helping relationship in a timely, planful, and deliberate way. How well you prepare in advance can stabilize clients' gains and increase their degree of insight and sense of independence. Take advantage of a head start. You have already previewed how clients may react to termination having observed their responses to your absences at vacation time, at the end of difficult interviews, or when changing or missing appointments. How clients typically handled these absences gives you a clue to how they will approach this permanent break.

Taking Leave

Take an active role in encouraging clients to think and talk about what goals have been accomplished, problems resolved, and risks taken. When you do, you enhance their ego and support their autonomy. Empathic affirmations lead to feelings of being valued and affirmed. Encourage clients to apply new learnings in assessing themselves and their progress. When you help them visualize how they will practice new behaviors in the future, they may venture to express a conditional "Good-bye." They may say, "I'm not ready for this," "Not yet," "Wait a while." Look closely at what they mean. Are they really saying, "Give me time to let go?" Reviewing the contract, as well as logs, inventories, and letters, written during your work, furnishes you and clients with tangible documentation of accomplishments. Ending does not have to be a unilateral, arbitrary decision because, from the outset, your contract contained mutually agreed upon goals, expectations, and guideposts, including those for termination. The contract makes termination less confusing and frustrating. It spells out in specific terms how changes might appear and identifies end-points to strive for. Rely on it for direction and remind clients about it.

During the termination process, clients say that they do not know how they feel or claim to have no feeling at all. Despite major steps forward in accepting responsibility for themselves and their actions, the threat of your "abandoning" them leaves them frightened and reluctant to follow through on their new course by themselves. Termination amplifies feelings of uncertainty, perhaps terror. When clients are not able to identify their feelings or accomplishments, name them yourself and invite their feedback. As you move through the pain of separation, model to clients that you yourself are able to plunge deeply into the intellectual, behavioral, and emotional effects of change.

Good-bye, Alan

The following excerpt from an actual interview with Alan, an eleven-year-old inner city school student, exemplifies some of the ideas highlighted above and shows that saying "good-bye," can have positive results.

> *Clinician:* You know Alan, we've only this and one more session before I leave. I'm feeling sad that I won't see you after next Friday. How about you?
>
> *Alan:* I'm happy . . . er, sad. I'm sad.

Cli: Have you ever lost a friend or had one move away?

Alan: Yeah, my old friends moved to the projects, and I moved to my grandmother's.

Cli: How did you feel when you didn't have them to play with?

Alan: My grandmother doesn't like me playing with hurt birds who can't fly no more. Would you like one of my puppies to keep, so you could remember me?

Cli: I'd like that but I can't keep a puppy where I live. It's not allowed. Once I had a pet turtle.

Alan: What happened to it?

Cli: It died and I felt real bad; I even cried because I cared a lot for it.

Alan: I had a goldfish that died. My grandmother gave it too much food and it died.

Cli: Gee, how'd you take that?

Alan: I don't know. I buried it in the yard.

Cli: When someone or something you care about leaves you, it's hard to take, like your goldfish and my turtle.

Alan: (nods affirmatively) I liked that goldfish and it went away.

Cli: I'm leaving soon, kind of feel bad about that, do you?

Alan: Could you stay here longer?

Cli: I'm afraid it's not possible but I'll remember you and me being friends, and having this time together.

Alan: When I go to the tutoring program, Bill takes me on trips.

Cli: You know you've made some changes this year, don't you Alan?

Alan: I can talk better, more words.

Cli: When I met you you were very quiet and shy, now you can say some things and express how you feel lots better; and your teacher says how good your math and writing are.

Alan: (listening)

Cli: When I've been in to see you in the classroom, I see your hand up a lot; that's quite a change from before.

Alan: I still like to hustle, but I come to school more now.

Cli: It's time to go now. I'll see you next week.

Alan: When will you come for me?

Cli: Same time as today, remember when that is?

Alan: Friday, right? After second period. (smiling)

Cli: I'll walk you back to class now.

Alan: I'm going to think about you.

Cli: I'm going to remember you too, Alan.

Guidelines for Leave-Taking

In leave-taking,

- focus on and highlight gains
- avoid tackling new problems
- validate and reinforce the client's problem solving capability
- relate to explicit and implicit positive statements and adaptations
- cite evidence of decisions, choices, and responsibility
- commend activity that exhibits motivation, self-direction, and self-control
- emphasize accomplishments and initiative taking
- comment on clients' worth and value
- consider future expectations
- express confidence in the client's future
- make clear the possibility of future help
- express interest and positive feelings for the client.

Guided exercises can assist you in helping clients to address separation issues. They can also foster self-awareness. In one exercise of fantasy gift exchanging, imaginary gifts are exchanged as a parting gesture. For example, I handed Sam, a 14-year-old male client, who had struggled and ultimately come to terms with overwhelming feelings of self-doubt, an imaginary can of "I cans" he had come to recognize. "I can do math problems," "I can ask for extra help in school when I need it," "I can score two foul shots in a row," and "I can graduate," were among these "cans." Sam offered me, in return, a Xerox copy of his imaginary "I will" poster listing such "wills" as, "I will go to high school," "I will talk to my mother more about her ignoring me," and "I will play on the basketball team."

In another exercise, clients draw a "map" of the helping process to illustrate symbolically any significant accomplishments that they find it difficult to state in words. Discussing the details and detours of their map of change opens avenues to verbal sharing. In another exercise, clients imagine departing in a car. Driving away, they peek into the rear view mirror to see what they are leaving behind and are asked to describe whatever feelings are evoked. They then shift the car into reverse and "return" to express what they would have regretted not having said had they left without this opportunity. Exercises such as these promote introspection, reflection, and open discussion.

GOOD-BYE, FAREWELL, AND BEYOND

Discuss plans and goals with clients; invite their recommendations and prescriptions for their own future. Do not hesitate to offer advice and observations to consolidate the experience you had together having successfully faced the unknown. Convey your confidence in their ability to meet what lies ahead of them without your continued presence.

Your final leave-taking can be extremely difficult, but can also be releasing. Be direct. Polite or mechanical platitudes get in the way of sharing intimate feelings. Prolonged hanging-on inhibits the release of emotions triggered by loss. Enable clients to release their feelings about separation by being genuine and honest yourself.

Saying "good-bye" is not a curse. Perhaps only through separation can clients become fully independent and developed. Think of "good-bye" as the departing blessing it originally meant. Say "good-bye" so that both of you are free to go on to the next "hello."

REFERENCES

Fox, Evelyn, et al. "The Termination Process: A Neglected Dimension in Social Work," *Social Work*, 41 (4), 1969.

Kübler-Ross, Elisabeth. *On Death and Dying*. NY: Macmillan, 1969.

Viorst, Judith. *Necessary Losses*. NY: Fawcett Gold Medal, 1986.

Webb, Nancy. "A Crisis Intervention Perspective On the Termination Process," *Clinical Social Work Journal*, 13 (4), 1985.

Index

Page numbers followed by f indicate figures.